JERRY HALL

My life in pictures

JERRY HALL

My life in pictures

Quadrille
PUBLISHING

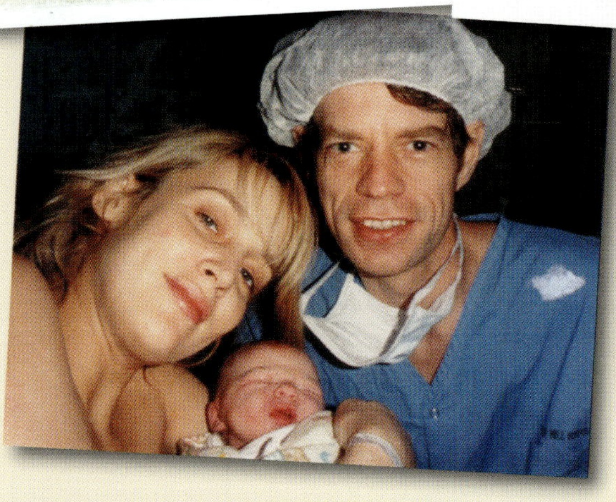

CONTENTS

INTRODUCTION

When I look back over my life, I can't help thinking how amazingly fortunate I have been. My childhood was certainly difficult – but if that poor little girl from Texas could have had even a glimpse of what would happen in her adult life she would have been amazed! From the moment I escaped to Paris at the age of 16 my life changed forever…

Professionally, I've been incredibly privileged to work with the greatest fashion photographers and designers of the past four decades. I've travelled the world modelling and acting in the theatre, on film and TV. Privately, I've met and in many cases become close to some of the most talented and influential people of these times. Of course, noone's life goes entirely according to plan and my love life, as everyone knows, has been complicated! But in the end I have a wonderful family: four beautiful children, an extended happy group of Stones ex-wives, girlfriends and step-children and, of course, my mother and four sisters to whom I am very close.

I have spent most of my life being a part of, and helping to create, beautiful images. So it seemed fitting, when I was invited to produce my autobiography, to base it around those images, professional and personal, which capture the most significant times in my past.

Bringing together the many different sides of my life for this book has been a wonderful and enriching experience which has brought back so many memories, most of them joyful, a few sad, and others funny, poignant and touching. I hope very much that you will enjoy reading it as much as I have enjoyed creating it.

Opposite: In my cowboy boots with my dog Butch. It could only be Texas.

1

TEXAS

Family history, surviving a difficult childhood

My story starts in Gonzales, Texas, a small town near the winding Guadeloupe River, between San Antonio and Austin, where I was born and spent the early years of my life with my Mama, Daddy and four sisters.

Many of the men in my life who have profoundly affected me were giant-sized characters – beginning with the first man in my life, my father John Printis Hall.

Brave men run in my father's family. He was one of fifteen children, but eight died from diphtheria. His mother, a Native American, died from typhoid fever when he was ten years old, and his father became an alcoholic, so Daddy left school at just ten years old and went to work to support his sisters.

As a young man of 21 at the outbreak of the Second World War, he was attached to General Patton's Third Army. He idolised Patton and frequently went way beyond the call of duty, and in return, Patton made him his master-sergeant and decorated him with medals for bravery.

Daddy married Mama, Marjorie Sheffield, in 1942, when he was home on leave. She was just 18 and a stunning beauty whose English and Irish ancestors had been amongst the early Texan settlers. Daddy was 24 and already a war hero and they were madly in love. But by the time Daddy got back from the war a few years later he had changed. His war had ended horribly. Patton had ordered him to take a platoon on a very dangerous mission and when some of the men refused, Daddy shot them. After the war he was court-martialled. It took 18 months, during which time he was not allowed to come home. He was found not guilty, but by the time he arrived back, hell, was he angry. And there was nothing my mother could do to make things better, other than to try and give him a son, and turn a blind eye to his violent mood changes.

As well as the readjusting to the humdrum routine of civilian life, Daddy had the added responsibility of bringing up a family. My eldest sister, Linda Nell, had been born in 1943, Cyndy and Rosemary followed and then, finally, Mama gave birth to us twins, on July 2, 1956. We were 8.5 pounds apiece, the biggest twins born in the state of Texas. Disappointed that we weren't boys, Daddy called us Terry Jaye and Jerry Faye.

Terry and I have always had an incredible bond. Because we were twins we were treated like a unit and when our parents wanted us they would call out 'Twins'. We always slept in the same bed and did everything together. We never fought, we nurtured and protected each other and shared our pain and grief. We had a special saying: 'Twins forever stick together', and we have done that through thick and thin.

Daddy used to go away for days at a time leaving us with no food to eat, while he tried to make a living as a professional gambler. Our poor mother was left alone with five small children in a rundown shack in a desolate, isolated area outside Gonzales with no water, car or help.

Aged six.

One day Daddy's uncle came over and saw the state we were living in. He packed us up and moved us to a house on a small farm in Gonzales. Mama got a night job at the hospital, as a records librarian. One night Daddy got drunk and came to our house with a pistol shooting it in the air. Linda was so scared she took us babies and hid with us under pillows in the closet.

Poor Linda, she didn't get a childhood. She had school all day and then had to look after us babies all night. She was only twelve but she was like a mother to us. Terry and I slept in the same crib, we wore cloth diapers and our bed would get very wet. That winter, when we were three months old, we got a cold and it turned into pneumonia. We almost died and had to spend several months in hospital.

For two years we were settled as a family and regular money was coming in. But everything was too normal, too mundane for Daddy. So he detonated our entire existence. First, he gambled the house and farm away in a poker game. And then, wracked with guilt and shame, he tried to kill himself. Unfortunately, he was no better at that than he was at poker; he got into our car and drove it at full speed into a brick wall. He succeeded only in breaking almost every bone in his body and losing a kidney, leaving Mama with five children to raise, no home, and a husband destined to spend a long time in hospital.

When Daddy was better and I was two years old, we moved to a little pink brick house in Mesquite outside Dallas. Daddy got a job driving dangerous chemicals around the country. He took uppers to stay awake, and when he came home his moods were dark. He would fly into rages and beat us girls one by one with his belt.

When Terry and I were four, we were sent to a nursery school. For some reason, the man who ran the nursery used to lock me up in a cupboard. Terry would sit outside the cupboard and put her finger in a crack to let me know I wasn't alone. One day our mother came early and found me in the cupboard. After that we never had to go there again.

We all started work as soon as we could. My first job was babysitting twin boys for a neighbor when I was 11. On weekends we would work at Cyndy's boyfriend Dub's stable. We broke horses, took kids for trail rides and cleaned out the stalls. Cyndy had become a Rodeo Queen, much fêted and celebrated and seriously glamorous too. Terry and I were her willing slaves, polishing her boots and starching her jeans. She liked them to stand up on their own and she had to lie on the floor while we zipped her in. We would run to the store to get her cigarettes and cherry coke.

Us twins, Mama and Daddy, all dressed up for Easter Sunday.

The rodeo was the biggest thing in town and we rode it every Friday and Saturday night when we got older. Terry and I used to ride 20 miles on our horses to get there. I used to ride in the Grand Entry with flags, doing formations. The cowboys would come from all over and they'd be so cute – real polite – but then they'd get drunk and rowdy.

While Cyndy was the Rodeo champion, my other sister Rosy had become a Dallas Cowboys Cheerleader. The Dallas Cowboys were our big pro football team, and Rosy was on TV, in the papers and considered very happening.

At fourteen I started working at Margery's Nursery School, looking after a room full of two-year-olds. I would go straight from school and stay until seven or eight at night, happy to be out of the house. Then I went to work in an old people's home where I wore a pink-and white-striped uniform and was called 'the candy striped girl'. My next job was at the Dairy Queen drive-in restaurant. But I got fired for giving away extra fries to my friends.

I had very little self-esteem. I never considered myself good-looking and at junior high, I often got bullied. They called me 'tall Hall', and the boys used to shout 'string bean'. I was the gawky, geeky kid who didn't quite cut it with the in-crowd.

We had very few books at home, but at some point my father had bought the complete works of Edgar Allan Poe. It was a *Reader's Digest* special and it soon became my companion. I memorised many of the poems and when Daddy was on the rampage, I would hide in the bushes out back and recite Poe's poems over and over while red ants bit my feet. I could always rely on Poe to get me through hard times and I developed a love of poetry as a result.

The idea of becoming a model started when I was invited to a house party one weekend by a friend whose parents had gone away. A boy there gave me some LSD, without telling me what it was. I locked myself in the bathroom and wouldn't come out. I didn't know what was happening to me – all I remember is that I looked at myself in the mirror and thought: 'You're really beautiful. You should become a model.' It was the first time that I had ever thought that.

Terry and I went to the Wendy Ward Charm School in our local shopping mall. There we learned to walk gracefully with a book on our heads, to turn on our heels and the proper way to sit with our knees together, crossed at the ankle and to take off our white gloves, one fingertip at a time. All very important stuff.

Our eldest sister Rosy had done the same course a few years before and she was now doing some selling and modelling at the Apparel Mart. Terry and I went to visit her and were offered some modelling work. We had to try on dresses for buyers and stand on a podium and dance to disco music. The clothes were disco, all sparkly and sexy. When we weren't dancing we had to give the buyers sandwiches and coffee. We were paid 25 dollars a day for a week's work, which was a fortune to us.

I went to see a model agent in Dallas, and she got me work at a fashion show; it was my first catwalk experience, but she said I was too tall and exotic for modelling in Dallas and told me that I should go to New York or Europe, where she thought I would get more work.

At 16 I got a job in a cafeteria in town, serving coffee. One day I was asked on a blind date. As my date, a couple of his friends and I set off, a car came really fast from the other direction and smashed into us. It was a sickening, terrifying collision. The couple in the front were really mashed up and my date was pretty badly hurt.

I was kept in hospital for a couple of days, and while I was there, my mother told the doctors that everyone in our family was allergic to penicillin. For some reason the message didn't get through; they gave me a shot of penicillin and I immediately went into convulsions. For a little while, it looked like I might die, but eventually I got better and the hospital offered me 800 dollars in compensation.

With the cash in my hand, I made a life-changing decision to go to France to be a model. All my sisters had left home as quickly as they could. Linda had married, Rosy had got pregnant, married and had Misty at just 17 and Cyndy left school and married Dub. When Terry got on the back of a friend's motorcycle and drove off to San Francisco, I just knew I had to go.

My French class had organised a school trip to Paris, which had been cancelled, as I was the only pupil who'd signed up for it. It was my disappointment after this that made me decide to go anyway – and along came the $800. The idea I had was to give modelling a year, and if it didn't work out, I would go back home and take up my scholarship to a local university.

Mama set to work making me a whole new wardrobe of old-style Hollywood clothes from Frederick's of Hollywood's catalogues. I remember one really wild dress, a red satin number that was skintight to the knees and then flared out. It had a little belt with rhinestone lips as a buckle: she was determined that her little girl would get noticed.

I left home in May, a few weeks before my seventeenth birthday, with a Eurail pass and a backpack full of Mama's home-made clothes, and flew to Paris.

Graduating from college.

Top left: Daddy's brothers and sisters. **Top right:** My great-grandfather. **Bottom left:** My great-grandmother. **Bottom right:** A photo of Pearl and Oscar Sheffield, my grandparents, taken in 1922. **Opposite:** My father's grandmother (on the Best family side).

My Pioneer Forebears

My family comes from all over the world; we're English, Irish, Scottish, Dutch, Choctaw and Cherokee Indian – quite a cocktail.

The first Dutch person in my father's family to come to Texas was Isaac Best and his was one of the first 300 families to settle. It was 1822 and Indian frontier country then. It wasn't even called Texas, it was part of Mexico. The Texans won it in a battle in Gonzales and the general who fired the first shot was General Beauregard; that's why Mick and I named our fourth child, Gabriel Luke Beauregard.

The Best family were strong people. They had to be brave and a little bit crazy to be going into these grasslands where previously Spanish ranchers and Comanche warriors had wrestled for control. They were a wealthy family with many horses and servants, and they had brought with them all their furniture and household goods. It's through our connection to the Best family that we are card-carrying members of The Daughters of The Republic of Texas.

The Best family's wealth was dispersed by the time it came down to my father's generation. My grandfather, Pop, still had a small piece of land, but no money and no one to work it. Our Uncle Charlie Miller – known as 'Killer Miller' – was one of the first Texas rangers, and his guns are now in the Texas Rangers Hall of Fame Museum in Waco. He helped to catch Bonnie and Clyde, and a lot of other famous outlaws.

Our father's sisters were called Lorene, Irene, Pearl, Sugar and Tootsie, and his brother was called Sonny. Sonny was a city cop in San Antonio, and his twin boys are now cops in Houston. Our cousin Lynn Sheffield was a sheriff in Gonzales and my nephew Jason Lehman, is a cop in Los Angeles. It must be in the blood.

Mama and Daddy

Daddy was a very good-looking man. With his mixture of European and Native American blood, he was dark-skinned, with strong, angular features and was said to resemble Clark Gable. Aware of his good looks, he wore his hat at a jaunty angle and had a keen eye for the ladies. Mama – Marjorie Nell Sheffield – was still at school when they married, just before he went off to fight in Europe. They were a striking couple: she was pale-skinned and statuesque, with thick black hair and a weakness for bright red lipstick.

Mama had an hour-glass figure and wherever we went, men would look at her and flirt with her. Daddy would get furious. Mama loved dancing and she looked so cute when she showed us how to do the jitterbug. She had seen *Gone with the Wind* over two dozen times and had a fantasy that she was Scarlett O'Hara. She often used to say 'I'll think about it tomorrow', just like her heroine.

When Daddy was away we used to do girly things with Mama. We would do beauty treatments using ingredients from the refrigerator; egg white masks and olive oil hair treatments. She would tell us to stand straight and be proud; she told us we were Amazon warrior women, and she would say how proud she was of us beautiful girls.

Her favourite thing was fishing. She would be so patient with us – helping us put worms on our hooks and taking the fish off the hook and gutting them for us. When we got back home, we would have a big fry-up.

Poor Mama was long-suffering. She and Daddy really loved one another when they married. But by the time they were reunited, the man she had married had sadly been brutalised by the war and his long incarceration.

Top left: Daddy kitted out in his millitary uniform and Mama with my eldest sister Linda. **Top right:** Daddy and the Hall girls. I'm the one below Mama, Terry's next to me and Linda, Cyndy, and Rosy make up the top row from left to right.

Bottom left: Terry and me outside Harwood, our first home. **Bottom right:** When we were seven years old, a neighbour who lived down the street gave Terry and me a surprise birthday party, with a cake and presents. We'd never had a party before.

Strangers' Funerals

My grandmother liked to go to strangers' funerals
Whenever she heard about one we would go
She used to say 'Well, so and so knew them'
And it's nice to have a good turn out

We drove in her old oldsmobile
While she was swattin' flys
To little white plankboard churches
In the middle of nowhere
Fifteen people in attendance

There was an open casket
We filed by
And looked at the dead waxen face
And listened to the sermon
Sometimes we cried

When we got back home
Our grandad was sitting
In the same spot on the porch
Rolling a cigarette
'You girls enjoy yourselves?'

Left: At Granny Pearl's house. **Opposite top:** Grandad feeding his chickens. **Opposite middle:** At a funeral with Granny, and a poem I wrote about the experience. Though it sounds strange, she loved going to funerals (even if she didn't know the deceased) and would often take us along for the ride. **Opposite bottom:** Granny and Grandad, Terry and me.

My Wonderful Grandparents

Every summer holiday we were sent to our grandparents for three months.

Pearl and Oscar Sheffield were our mother's parents and we loved being with them, because at their home we could be like a normal family. They never raised their voices or seemed to have a cross word to say to one another, they always seemed to enjoy each other's company. We had meals together at regular times and we had conversations. Pearl loved playing cards and dominoes, and we would play and laugh together. Although she was very religious and strict, she was also fair and we knew where we stood with her.

Their home was a little wooden plank-board house consisting of one bedroom, a living room and kitchen, and a big wrap-around wooden covered porch where Linda got to sleep on a bed, while us four youngest slept on a pallet in the front room.

Granny was always complaining that Mama hadn't taught us anything and would ask us 'How did we think you are gonna get a man?' She taught us to cook and bake bread, how to mend and sew and eight different kinds of needlepoint, which was extremely useful for Terry and me as we always ended up getting all the hand-me-downs.

We used to love to go with our Grandad to give the chickens their molasses. We'd sit on the back of his flatbed truck and stop at each little chicken house and pour out their feed and some molasses syrup. It was sweet and sticky and we'd lick it off our fingers.

Rodeo Girls

My aunts, Daddy's sisters, were very beautiful and a bit wild. Aunt Pearl had lost all her hair, through diphtheria, and she had wigs of every colour. We loved trying on her wigs and would howl with laughter at the way we looked in them.

We had a little gang of girlfriends and we often spent the weekends at our friend Karen McRae's house. Karen had a poster of Mick Jagger on her closet door, we all thought he was cute. We started the 'Try Anything Once Club', goading each other into dares such as riding a cow, or a wild horse, or climbing a tall tree. But at 15 we discovered *Cosmopolitan* magazine and decided that we had to lose our virginity. None of us had a boyfriend, so Karen and I set our sights on the star bull-rider at the local rodeo. We organised a dance at his father's barn and, flushed with cheap wine, Karen disappeared with him into the hayloft. He invited me out the next night and afterwards we went back to the hayloft where, with the rain coming through the roof and splashing on my face, I lost my virginity. I had my boots on – cowgirl was definitely the look in those days – and it was neither romantic nor special.

My first real boyfriend was Jim Murdoch. He was 18, with dark hair and olive skin. He rode saddle broncs at the rodeo and would walk 20 miles to sit on the porch and play chess with me. I was heartbroken when he said he had fallen in love with another girl.

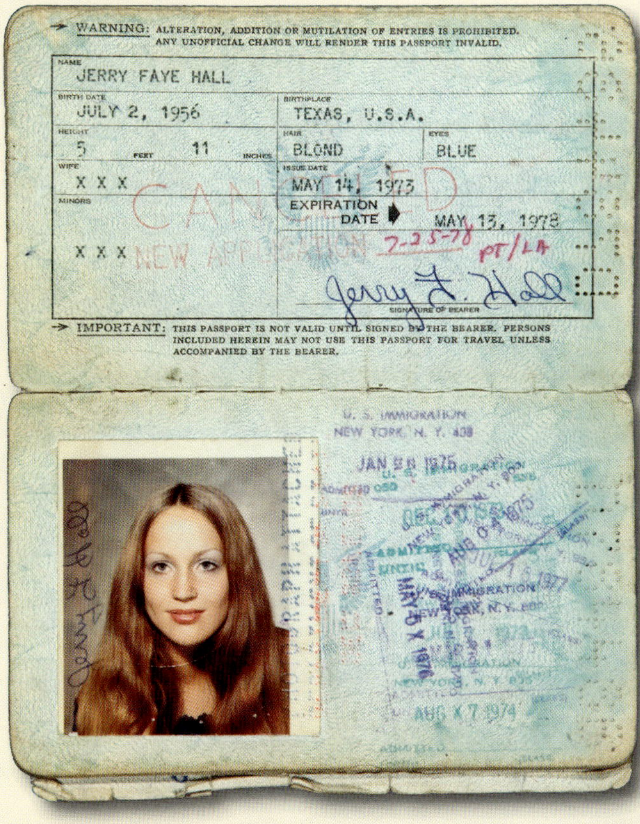

Opposite left: Me wearing one of Aunt Pearl's colourful wigs. **Opposite right:** Messing around with Rosy and Terry. **Top left:** The Try Anything Once Club at the carnival. **Top right:** My first boyfriend, Jim Murdoch.

Bottom left: Terry and me with our dog Prissy and an assortment of cats. **Bottom right:** My very first passport, which I got especially for my trip to Paris. The photo here is from my high school graduation.

Left: A very early modelling job, and some very crazy hair!

2

PARIS

Becoming a model, working with Helmut Newton and Yves St Laurent

When I arrived in Paris I was overwhelmed by a combination of panic and exhilaration. I didn't know a thing about France, except what I'd learned from the films I had watched with my French class at school, amongst them those by the legendary filmmaker Luis Buñuel. I adored his films; they were so stylised and dark and interesting, and totally unlike the Hollywood fodder which was being put out by the American studios in the early seventies. I was sure that if it was anything like the films, then Paris must be wonderful.

It was a sunny May morning when I took my first taxi ride through the city. The streets were still wet from a light shower and I rolled down the window and breathed in the heady smell – a mixture of rain, dust and chestnuts being roasted by the sidewalk vendors. As we drove up to the Arc de Triomphe, I took out my Kodak instamatic camera and started taking photos. The beauty of the impressive buildings, and the sensuous statues and fountains that we passed thrilled me.

I checked into a youth hostel, unsure what to do next. A few days later, with my backpack and my Euro rail pass, off I went to Saint-Tropez. I was excited about heading to the South of France as my mother had told me the Riviera was *the* place to go and I had spent way too much money buying a beautiful pink metallic crochet bikini and a pair of ridiculous, giant pink and silver platform shoes with cork wedges.

On my first morning on the beach, I must have stood out from the crowd; 16 years old, six foot tall, long blonde hair and in my shocking pink ensemble!

I lay on the beach and when mid morning came; I went off to the bathroom. On the way back, a man stopped me and asked, 'would you like to be a model in Paris?' I tried to play it cool, and took his card. I phoned him that night and he offered to pay my fare back to Paris where he said he would put me in an apartment with some other models. And that's how it all started. I couldn't believe I'd been asked to be a model on my very first day on the beach.

I went back to Paris and moved into a flat with a couple of other girls and the agency started sending me for modelling jobs. One night my flatmate Tom Cashin introduced me to the fashion illustrator Antonio Lopez.

Originally from Puerto Rica, he had lived in the States and then come to live in Paris, where he was doing illustrations for magazines.

Antonio became a great friend. He taught me how to model and a lot about fashion and photography. His drawings intrigued me, and I developed an interest in the history of fashion and photography. I read up on the subject, studying the many fashion and photography books in Antonio's studio. I was captivated by the models' poses and copied them for hours, using a full-length mirror. Oddly, my naivety increased my confidence for I imagined that I could be the best model in the world, if there was such a thing!

I led a hectic existence, going to see people about modelling jobs, posing for Antonio and studying my craft, as well as going out at night a lot.

Everywhere I went I seemed to meet famous and interesting people. I used to have tea with Salvador Dali and his wife Gaia. He asked me to do a film with him at his house in Spain. He wanted me to be nude with just a white veil over my head, running through his sculpture garden. I said 'no' as I had promised my Mama I wouldn't pose nude. I had dinner with King Vidor, the former movie director, and his daughter one night. I used to have lunch at La Coupole; it was the in place to eat. I once went there all dressed up in Mama's sexy glam clothes, borrowed my agent's Great Dane and put a rhinestone collar on it. I was having coffee and got talking to an older couple sitting next to me. They turned out to be Jean-Paul Sartre and Simone de Beauvoir. I knew who they were, because I had watched their programme about existentialism on TV and I also loved his book *Being and Nothingness*, exploring our inner and outer selves.

Jean-Paul and Simone invited me to lunch, along with my twin sister Terry, who had come over to stay with me for a while. They loved hearing about our small town and the rodeo.

By that time we were living in a little hotel called The Hotel Crystal and Grace Jones moved in with us for a while. We shared a room; it had twin beds on one side and a single bed on the other and was divided by a curtain. Grace had just arrived in Paris hoping to be a model and she didn't have much money or a place to live. We thought she was fun and told her to move in. We also used to hang out with Bellina Hall and Pat Cleveland. Bellina was singing and dancing in transvestite cabaret, and Pat was a model – I thought she was the best there was. We used to put on little cabaret shows for friends in our hotel room, singing songs like, *Three little girls from Little Rock*. Terry and I kept telling Grace that she should be a singer; she had such a beautiful voice. Antonio introduced Grace to Jean-Paul Goude, the photographer. He took wonderful photographs of her, amazing iconic images that celebrated her African roots, and Grace eventually moved in with him.

Terry and I kept getting kicked out of hotels for making too much noise. The Hotel Crystal was followed by Le Montana and then La Louisiana. Whichever hotel we were in, we always had breakfast everyday at the Café de Flore, the place to be. Eventually Terry and I got our own apartment and for our first dinner party we invited all our friends, and served instant mash potatoes and frozen oven-baked French fries, with lots of red wine. Our friends laughed so much at our awful first attempt at cooking.

Our apartment was on a street with a large graveyard across the road. Three Iranian students lived upstairs; nice guys who said 'hello' if we passed them on the stairs. One night after a dinner out, we took the metro home. That meant walking past the graveyard which always gave us the creeps. When we realised a man was walking behind us, Terry and I picked up our pace – and so did the man. We ran through our front door which had no lock, and up the winding metal stairs and the man followed us and grabbed at our ankles. We screamed and I took off one of my high heels and hit him with it. Our Iranian friends came out and chased the guy off, but we were so shaken we decided to move out.

Terry didn't like modelling and only stayed a few months before she went back home to Texas. But for me, Paris was everything I wanted. By that time I had got a good agent and been introduced to Helmut Newton, who gave me my first big break. I was appearing on the covers of magazines like *Elle*, *20 Ans*, *Stern*, French *Vogue* and Italian *Vogue*, and getting a lot of pictures in the fashion news. I was always amazed when I passed a news-stand and saw my face.

I was also catwalk modelling and doing several of the big couture fashion shows – for Yves Saint Laurent, Madame Grey and Valentino, amongst others. I became a favourite of the catwalk photographers because I would often stop a few feet before the end of the runway and pose for them. Bill Cunningham, who was a friend of Antonio's and a great reportage photographer, would shout, 'Go get 'em, Tex'.

Hanging out with Grace and Antonio.

It was such an exciting time. Wherever I went with Antonio, everyone would look and whisper my name, which I found unnerving at first.

Everything was about how you looked. I often hated the ruthlessness and shallowness of some people, but I found

I could rise above it by making my exterior my own work of art. I threw myself into studying art, fashion, and beauty. I became obsessed and ruthless about my creation – me. I tried every shape of eyebrow, until I finally got the right one; I had Marlene Dietrich's thin pencil line, Joan Crawford's thick brush-up brows, until I settled in the end for a high-arched brow, thick at the beginning and finishing in an elongated line. I found that with practice I could train my face muscles, suck in my cheekbones, drop my jaw and arch one eyebrow; I became an expert at the haughty look. I was obsessed with Italian film director Luchino Visconti's films and the way he used total artifice as a way to the truth and I tried to emulate that.

The Hall twins a long way from Texas.

I worked with great make-up artists at Yves Saint Laurent when I started doing his fashion shows – Jose Louis and Jacques Clement – and I watched and copied their make-up. I felt like a painter with my easel, painting my face meticulously and trying to imitate what they had done. I also worked with the famous hairdresser Alexandre de Paris. He had done Elizabeth Taylor's hair for the film Cleopatra and he went every morning to the Bois de Boulogne to do the Duchess of Windsor's hair. He was a magician who sculpted my hair into the most wonderful shapes.

Antonio knew everyone and everywhere we went he would introduce me to extraordinary people from the worlds of fashion, film and art. One of the people I met was the artist Andy Warhol. Andy loved Antonio's fashion illustrations and would come to the studio to admire his work. Andy was sweet and gentle and we became lifelong friends. He was always with his sidekick, Fred Hughes. Fred was Texan and, with his slicked back shiny black hair and fitted, elegant suits, he was a beautiful dandy and one of the funniest men I have ever met. They both said I must come to New York and they would help launch my career there.

I had been in Paris less than a year and a half when *Newsweek* did a story with a photo of me, saying I was the new model taking Paris by storm. By then I had changed agencies and was finally starting to make money.

I was so surprised at being famous and a little bit frightened too. People had always looked at me, because I was tall, but now strangers kept recognizing me and kept coming up and talking to me.

With all the attention I was getting in Paris, word spread to New York. Eileen Ford, who owned Ford Models, invited me to dinner one night. She asked me to come and model in New York and said I could live in her house. I accepted.

Becoming a Model

The agent who signed me up in Paris – I always called him 'The Tunisian' – gave me an advance on my earnings. He took the money out of his sock, that's where he kept it! He paid me 1000 Francs (about 200 dollars) for a seven year contract for the world; models nowadays would be getting paid millions for that kind of contract. But in those days there were a lot of crooks and sleazy types in the modelling world and I was very naïve.

My agency billed me as 'La Nouvelle Veruschka' – she was a German countess who had been one of the greatest models in the sixties. They also wanted me to change my name, because it sounded too much like a boy. They suggested calling me 'Texas' or 'Tex', but I said no.

In the early days I pounded the pavements and used the metro all day on model 'go-sees', meeting people for jobs. And within a week, I had my first – a poster for a petrol station in which I posed in a suggestive manner holding a petrol pump! My next job was my very first magazine cover shoot, although it was only a knitting magazine. And after that I started getting better jobs, and made the covers of *Elle* and *Vogue*. I couldn't believe how quickly things took off and how lucky I was.

Above: My first modelling card.
Opposite: One of my first modelling jobs for French magazine 20 ans.

Antonio Lopez: My Mentor

I first met Antonio in the Club Sept in Paris. I was wearing gold satin with lots of glitter and feathers and he was wearing a white satin jacket and a red beret. Antonio was a brilliant fashion illustrator, he asked me to pose for him and we became very close. Then after my sister Terry went back to Texas I moved in with Antonio and we became lovers for a while.

Antonio knew everyone, and everywhere we went he introduced me to people from the world of fashion, film and art. He was friends with Andy Warhol and when he came to town we had dinner together at the Club Sept. Andy had been a very successful commercial artist and fashion illustrator, who had won awards from the Art Director's club, before he had become the Pop Art media superstar of the sixties.

Antonio taught me so much about make-up and style. When I got to Paris I was wearing blue eye shadow from eyelash to eyebrows, pink right up my cheeks and pink lipstick. Antonio would spend two hours making me up, with eye-liner, false eyelashes and plucked eyebrows. After that I always made my eyebrows arched, the way he drew them. I used to sit for hours with his drawings of me and copy the make-up.
He taught me how to pose, what to do with my hands and how to stay still and look graceful and elegant.

He used to laugh at my poses and my outfits. I was still wearing my mother's Frederick's of Hollywood outfits – I thought they were chic, but Antonio taught me that that they were camp instead. I'd been camping it up all along and I didn't know it.

Antonio always brought a lot of originality and humour into his work. He never stopped drawing and experimenting with different styles and he produced hundreds of drawings. Some of the drawings he did of me, Grace Jones and other models went into his book, *Antonio's Girls*, which came out in 1982. A few years after we met we went to Jamaica with Norman Parkinson to shoot pictures for English *Vogue*, Parks photographed Antonio drawing me on the beach. I loved the way he drew me, he was the only person who ever got my mouth just right.

Left: I love this drawing Antonio did of me as a mermaid – it's elegant, vibrant and full of movement.
Opposite: Posing for Antonio on the beach in Jamaica for English Vogue, photographed by Norman Parkinson.

Mobil
Unleaded

ald's
SERVED

Winston

EXXON

Opposite: Antonio's photos of our Texan road trip. Right: The most beautiful Valentine's card I have ever received. Below: Striking a pose.

When we were living in New York I took Antonio to my cousin Jo-Nell's wedding. We drove right across the US to Texas and he took dozens of pictures of me in front of the signs we passed along the way. I think they're wonderful – very artistic and very American – they remind me of paintings by Ed Roche. Antonio was brilliant; his drawings appeared in *Vogue*, *Harper's Bazaar* and the *New York Times* and his work was exhibited all over the world.

We were only lovers for a short while, but we stayed close friends and I was devastated when he died in 1987 at the age of only 44.

Helmut Newton: My Big Break

Opposite: My big break, an amazing shoot that got me the cover of Vogue Beauty. After this shoot, my modelling career really took off.

In Paris in 1973, Helmut Newton was the top photographer. He was producing haunting, seductive, shocking photographs for French *Vogue* and *Photo* magazine. Helmut's photos (which are reproduced here from original tearsheets) were both distinctive and stylised. There was a buzz about his work; he was inspiring not only to photographers, but also to filmmakers, artists and fashion designers and I longed to work with him. Helmut had created a world inhabited by powerful, glamorous, sexy women. He had been brought up in Berlin in the thirties and early memories of his glamorous mother's style of chiffon and lace, her furs and perfume influenced him.

Helmut was part-Jewish and had escaped from Germany during the war. He moved to Australia, where he met his wife, June. They had married young, and were very much in love when I met them 26 years later.

I first met Helmut at the Club Sept, the happening club in Paris in the early seventies, where we were introduced by my friend Antonio Lopez. I wore a gold satin forties vintage suit and a blue ostrich feather boa from the Mesquite Sewing Centre. My waist-length hair had been pin-curled, producing a thick wave and I wore red lipstick and gold glitter eye shadow. Helmut asked me to pose for him for *Photo* magazine the next day and I was thrilled. I arrived at his studio at 11am – no-one started work early in those days. We grabbed a taxi and went to Pigalle; the slightly seedy part of town, where there were a lot of sex shops. We stopped at one and Helmut and the sales assistant chose a lot of S&M outfits and handed them to me to try on behind a curtain. They were mostly bits of leather and harness and I felt very uneasy about them and kept saying, 'No, they're too small'. Finally, I tried on a few things that fitted and Helmut chose some whips and handcuffs to go with them.

We went back to the studio where he had a hair stylist and make-up artist Jacques Clement waiting. Helmut's wife June was there, she was very friendly and I started to feel a bit more relaxed about it all. Helmut was very particular about my hair and make-up; he wanted me to have matt red lipstick, dark eyes and forties Veronica Lake-style hair.

VOGUE
PARIS
F 12
SPÉCIAL
BEAUTÉ
automne-hiver 74-75
beauté
sur
mesure
selon
votre âge
et
votre vie
pour
cet hiver

Jacques Clement transformed me; I looked like a Hollywood star from the old black-and-white movies that I had grown up dreaming about. My hair was perfection; it's still my favourite hairstyle. Helmut was pleased, but very particular. To complete the look, he said, my fingernails needed to be painted red.

When I was ready I was given very high heels, fishnets, a leather pointed bra, leather hot pants and waist clincher. I went on the set and Helmut gave me a long bullwhip, which I proceeded to crack. I didn't feel that Helmut was interested in me sexually, but I could see that he was clicking into some fantasy of his own. He seemed very pleased with me, but didn't want me to smile or laugh. The more cross and haughty I looked, the more excited he got. We did a few other outfits with various whips and paddles and handcuffs, and then he gave me something that looked like a horse bridle to put on next. I burst into tears and he looked shocked and said, 'Please don't cry, I hate it when models cry, you're ruining your make-up'. He asked me what was wrong and I said, 'I don't want to do porn – I want to be in *Vogue*'. He said, 'Silly girl, this isn't porn, it's art'. Then he said, 'If *Vogue* is what you want, we will do that next'.

He kept his word. A few weeks later we did the cover of French *Vogue Beauty*. Helmut also did an extraordinary shoot for *Vogue Beauty*, of me with a raw steak on my eye – the idea was to show readers how to cure a black eye, and it made for a very dramatic picture.

Helmut, June and I became very good friends. We worked together for over 30 years and travelled the world together, working in different locations for French and American *Vogue*. We had a wonderful, warm relationship and enjoyed many terrific dinners together. And we produced some beautiful photographs.

Above: Filled with sexual tension, aggression even, this polaroid shows just what made Helmut's photos so very special. **Opposite:** A striking picture (reproduced from an original tearsheet) of me for Vogue Beauty with a steak against my eye. This was June Newton's idea, it came from her fridge and they had it for supper later that night!

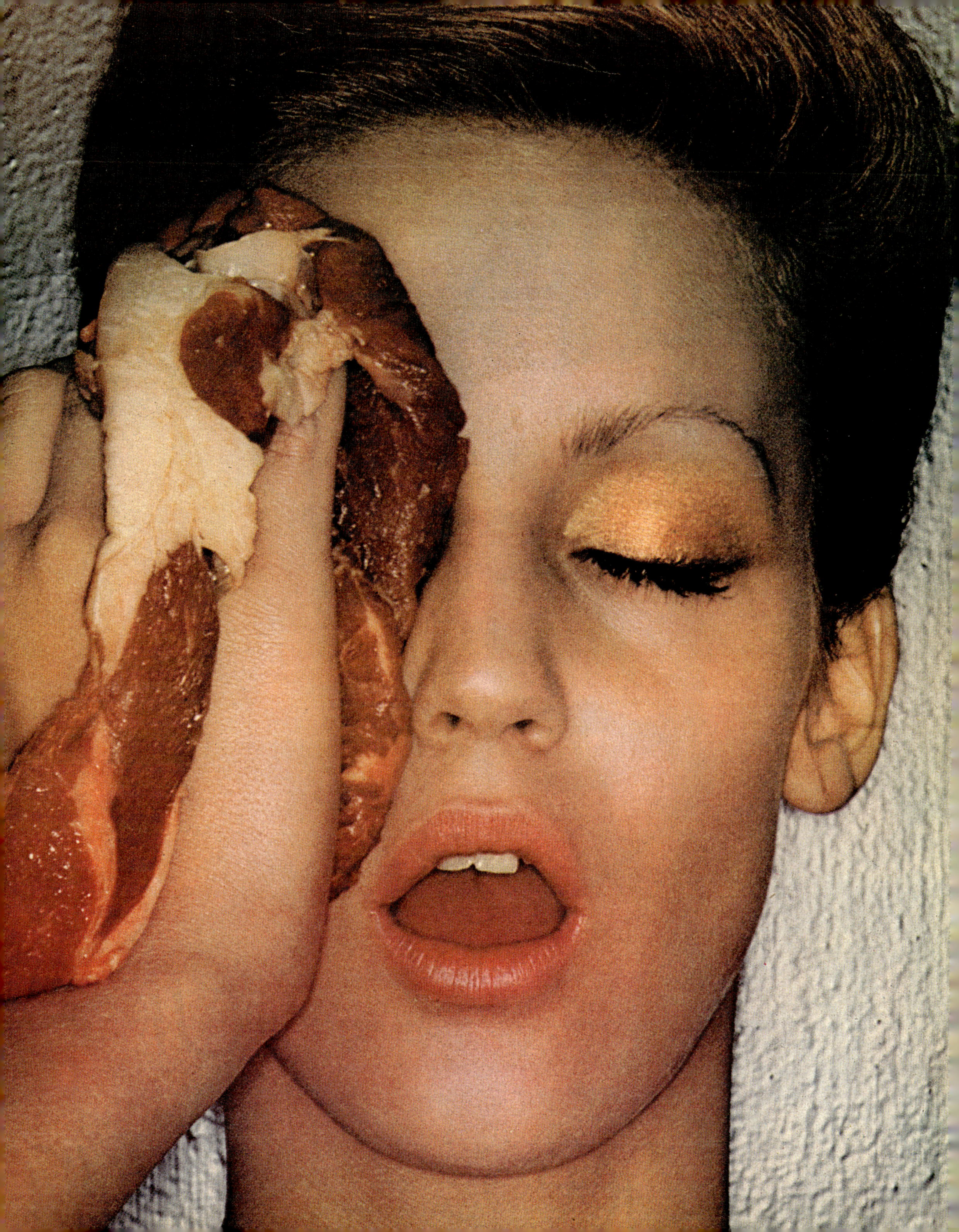

AIR REAM
Ran

I always understood instinctively exactly what Helmut wanted in his photos. He liked his women strong, haughty and cruel. He loved it when I would claw, bite and spit on my poor fellow model, be it male or female. I saw a lot of models cry when working with Helmut, but I never made that mistake again. Helmut liked to provoke his models, make them angry and I knew that I had to produce the goods if I didn't want to be insulted and humiliated in the name of art.

When I was living in New York we did a shoot in Florida for American *Vogue*, with American model Lisa Taylor and I in Rudi Gernreich cutaway thong swimsuits. We posed on the beach, like Amazonian women, facing in opposite directions, and I gave Lisa my long hair to pull. It looked like very stylised wrestling and the resulting dramatic photo was used across a double page spread and is in many of Helmut's books.

Following pages: Lisa Taylor and me in Florida for French Vogue, 1975 (reproduced from an original tearsheet). **Below left:** Giving Helmut something to think about! Posing down by the beach after the same shoot. **Below right:** Winding down post-shoot with Polly Mellen, Lisa Taylor and makeup artist Rick Gallant. **Opposite:** Another great image, this one shot in Miami for American Vogue, 1974 (reproduced from an original tearsheet).

It was on a trip to Los Angeles with Helmut Newton, to do a swimwear shoot for American Vogue that we bumped into Arnold Schwarzenegger. He just happened to be staying in the same hotel, we got talking and Helmut had the idea of asking Arnold to be in one of the pictures. He was then in his early thirties and was the greatest bodybuilder in the world, having won the Mr Universe title and then the greatest title of all, Mr Olympia, six times in a row. Helmut wanted all us models on the shoot to look as bored as possible while Arnie stood there, flexing his muscles and trying to attract our attention.

Opposite: Caesar's Palace, Las Vegas, American Vogue, 1975

OPIUM
pour celles qui adorent Yves Saint Laurent.

Yves Saint Laurent: A Very Special Designer

When the film *Belle du Jour* came out in 1967 the fashion world was electrified by the fact that Yves Saint Laurent had designed all the dresses. In this scandalous erotic film, Catherine Deneuve plays a bourgeois housewife who has a secret life as a daytime prostitute, just for fun. It gave a double life to luxury clothes.

When I arrived in Paris, I was invited to model for Yves Saint Laurent and then given a contract to model his designs. I appeared in all his catwalk shows, and was thrilled to be asked to do the first photo campaign for his new perfume, Opium. The photographs were taken by Helmut Newton (and are reproduced here as magazine tearsheets) and the campaign was a huge success.

Yves was a genius and a charming fragile man. I got to know him well, because as part of my contract I had to attend high profile parties and events with him – always dressed in couture YSL, of course.

SAINT LAURENT
rive gauche
ABRAHA

Left: Stepping out onto the catwalk and striking a pose in YSL at Paris Fashion Week. **Below:** Yves putting the final touches to my outfit before sending me onto the runway. **Opposite:** Modelling a white satin gown and the famous 'Le Smoking' tuxedo at Yves' final show in Paris, 2002.

Yves always made you feel as if your opinion mattered. He used to call his design studio 'The House of Love'. He wanted to know, did you like the outfit? Did you feel good in it? He was very sensitive; if you thought a dress might look better slightly different, all you had to do was hold it or lift it a certain way and he would pick up on that and change it and in that way you felt you were contributing and collaborating. He loved women and he wanted you to be really happy and to think that your outfit was just the best.

I modelled in all of his shows. The last catwalk show I did, in 2002, was a retrospective of his work in Paris. Yves had all the models who'd appeared in his clothes throughout the years, Catherine Deneuve, Veruschka, Claudia Schiffer, Naomi Campbell and many, many others. We showed clothes from the sixties, seventies and eighties. His health was really failing by then and he died a few years later, but I will always remember him as a lovely man.

Left: Barbara Allen and me strutting our stuff in downtown Manhattan.

3

NEW YORK

Hitting the big time, travelling the world

I arrived in New York in late 1974 wearing mink. While I was in Paris I had saved my money in a shoebox under my bed, and before I left I spent it all on a floor-length silver fox-trimmed mink cape from Revillon. I put it straight on and walked down the Champs-Élysées, admiring myself in all the shop windows.

Antonio went back to the States around the same time, so at first I stayed with him in the Chelsea Hotel. It was full of artists and drug addicts, which was an interesting combination. I met the fashion designer Charles James who lived there – he had the most amazing ball gowns that he had designed in the fifties, and I modelled them for museum exhibitions of his work.

One night robbers came into the hotel with machine guns. They seized people out of the elevator and took them to a room where they raped the women. I was in my room alone watching TV and didn't hear anything. When I learned about it the next day, I decided to take up Eileen Ford's offer of a home with her and her husband Jerry.

The Fords had a beautiful town house on the Upper East Side, and a country home in Connecticut. Eileen took over the role of surrogate mother and as I was only 18, she gave me a midnight curfew. It felt a bit odd, as I had been making my own way since I was 16, but I liked the feeling of safety that being part of her family gave me. Each weekend I piled into the station wagon with her kids and we set off for the country.

In Paris I had worked with the great photographers such as Helmut Newton, Guy Bourdin, Jeanloup Sieff and Sarah Moon. This was the fashion world's equivalent of graduating from Yale with honours and I went straight to the top of the agency's list. There were no more 'go sees' for me, I was booked every day. I worked for American *Vogue*, did beauty and fashion ads with Irving Penn, shot a Revlon campaign with Richard Avedon and was photographed for *Cosmopolitan* covers by Francesco Scavullo. The Fords would book several jobs for the same day and then choose the best for me and cancel the others. I also made the cover of Andy Warhol's *Interview* magazine, which was considered very cool.

I loved being busy and was happy to work non-stop. I started doing television commercials for Coca Cola and Olympus Cameras, and I also did the first Calvin Klein jeans print and television ads with Richard Avedon.

I travelled a lot too, going on location to shoot editorials for American *Vogue* and *Harper's Bazaar*, often working with other models who were well-known at that time. I went to Mexico with Patti Hansen, to Florida with Lisa Taylor and the Caribbean with Cheryl Tiegs who brought along her boyfriend, photographer Peter Beard. I also worked a lot with Christie Brinkley and Beverly Johnson, Iman and Roseanne Vela, another model from Texas. Sometimes we all worked together doing group shots. They were all really lovely girls and even though modelling was a competitive environment, we were all friendly. Despite our hectic schedules there was a lot of partying going on. We often went to New York's hottest club, Studio 54, to dance the night away, but no matter how late we partied, the next day we girls would be up and ready to go – we were very professional and serious about our work.

While a handful of models were very successful, the same was true of the photographers. There were a few who were the best of their generation; Francesco Scavullo, Richard Avedon, Irving Penn, Bill King, Rico Puhlmann, Hiro, Helmut Newton, Norman Parkinson, Albert Elgort and Albert Watson and of course the models and photographers got to know each other well.

Work New York-style was a shock to the system after Paris. In Paris we all considered ourselves artists and didn't start work till 11am, and then had big breaks for proper, delicious lunches. In New York, it was early starts and a quick sandwich for lunch. The work was much harder and the clothes were often less glamorous.

I soon realised that being a model in America was more than just producing beautiful pictures; it was selling a dream. And it was a ruthless business – I was told I would last five years if I was lucky.

After six months, living with the Fords was getting a bit difficult, what with the curfew and the housekeeper taking my telephone calls. They had been so kind to me, but it was time to be more independent, so I moved into an apartment with my girlfriend Alvenia Bridges, a fellow model. We first tried a loft way downtown, where we slept on tatami mats, but it had no heating and was freezing cold. So we got an apartment in Greenwich Village where we did a lot of yoga, and read *The Prospering Power of Love*, a book about positive thinking.

Alvenia and I had a gang of girlfriends in the Village that we hung out with. Liz Derringer, who was married to the rock star guitarist Rick Derringer, and actress sisters Geraldine and Maria Smith. The five of us often went clubbing and had dinners together. Alvenia and I were both over six feet tall with our heels on and Geraldine, Maria and Liz were all very tiny girls so I'm sure we looked funny together, but we had a lot of fun.

Once I took Geraldine, Liz and Alvenia home to Texas to meet my family. I hadn't been back for a while, and it was good to see them. We all stayed in our little house in Mesquite and I took the girls to the Mesquite Rodeo, all dressed up like cowgirls. We had a great time – they couldn't believe how cute the cowboys were.

It was great fun living in the Village. Every morning we had coffee at the Italian cafés. We shopped for vintage clothes and I started to collect a Fiestaware dinner service. I loved its beautiful colours and shapes; it had been around since the thirties but wasn't made any more, so finding pieces was always exciting.

My sister Cyndy, who by this time was a champion rodeo rider, arrived in town to ride bulls at Madison Square Garden and she came to stay with us – along with three guys who rode the bulls with her. They wanted to stay for a couple of days and Alvenia was worried because our apartment was so small; we only had two bedrooms. But they said they would sleep on the floor and promised to be quiet and we agreed because they were awfully cute. They left a lot of beer bottles around the place when they went, but they also gave me and Alvenia a pair of jeans each that fitted so perfectly we couldn't believe it.

At this time I was appearing on hundreds of magazine covers for publications all over the world and I travelled a lot doing catwalk shows for the designers' collections. I would travel to Milan and be in 30 fashion shows a week, then go to Paris for 35 shows a week, before heading on to Japan for their shows and then straight back to New York to do another 30. It was a gruelling non-stop schedule, but I loved it.

I was so lucky to have worked with so many of the most gifted and talented artists and photographers of the day. I did a lot of swimsuit shoots, having been girls' leg wrestling champion back in Texas and ridden horses all my life as well as being a keen dancer – I was very strong and had good muscle tone.

I cannot tell you the thrill of working for a great artist or photographer and having a kind of telepathy, a symbiotic partnership, striving and working together to achieve a desired effect. The mutual excitement was breathtaking. The greater the artist or photographer, the greater the possibility of achieving a lasting iconic image; a true work of art.

With the legendary American Vogue editor Diana Vreeland at a Christie's preview.

At that time the greatest living photographer was Irving Penn. I first worked with him for American Vogue when he was in his fifties and I was eighteen. His wife, Lisa Fonssagrives, was his receptionist. I couldn't believe it; she had been the most beautiful Vogue model of the forties and fifties, the first supermodel and the first model to make the cover of *Time* magazine. She was Swedish, stunning and fearless, an ex-dancer, who had hung perilously from the iron spars of the Eiffel Tower for Erwin Blumenfeld, disrobed for Horst and parachuted over the Paris skyline for Jean Moral. I was blown away by meeting her.

Whenever I entered Penn and Lisa's studio they gave me a warm welcome. I felt I was entering the inner sanctum of evolved photographic art and that anything could happen. I had goose bumps on my arms at the opportunity to do something great,

to collaborate in making a stunning image that could make people's heart skip. It was the absolute pinnacle of model heaven.

I also loved posing for artists, having started as a model for Antonio's fashion illustrations. I always loved dressing up and posing and Antonio loved drawing and taking photos of me. I consider him to be the greatest fashion illustrator ever. He was so ahead of his time – his finger was on the pulse of every new movement. As well as posing for Antonio, I was painted by Andy Warhol and then by Ed Ruscha, Francesco Clemente and Paul Benney.

New York was fun – I loved the clubs, the fashion designers, and the parties with friends. My time there was a non-stop whirlwind. One of my good friends was Diana Vreeland, the former editor of American Vogue who had gone on to run the Metropolitan Museum of Art's Costume Institute. We used to hang out together at Studio 54.

One of Diana's protégées was Polly Mellen, who became the editor at American *Vogue*. I was shocked when Polly told me one day that *Vogue* wanted me to have a Dutch boy haircut; a short bob with a fringe, or they wouldn't work with me anymore. They said if I cut my hair they would put me on two covers and do twelve pages with Irving Penn. It was tempting. But my hair was so much a part of who I was. I was the first model to have really long hair and it had worked for me – I felt it was modern and strong, vital and yet still feminine, so I refused.

Soon after that I went to Jamaica to do a shoot for English *Vogue*. Norman Parkinson was doing the photographs and Grace Coddington, a former model who later worked with Anna Wintour on American *Vogue* and starred with her in the film *The September Issue*, was our stylist. I brought Antonio along for the trip, and Grace suggested putting him in the pictures with me, which produced some wonderful images.

For one of the shots Parks put me on a horse in a billowing blue dress without a saddle. The horse was startled by the camera noise and took off, throwing me into the wooden post of a barbed wire fence. I fractured my tail bone and got barbed wire cuts on my bottom. Norman ran over and said, 'I thought you said you were from Texas and could ride'. My dress was torn and I was bleeding, but he put me straight back on another horse and did the photos.

The photos that Parks took in Jamaica were sensational and produced two English *Vogue* covers. British rock star Bryan Ferry of Roxy Music saw them and called Eileen Ford to ask me to do the cover of his new album. He flew me to London and picked me up himself in an old-fashioned Daimler. I took one look at his elegant, handsome face and forgot all about New York.

Francesco Scavullo

Scavullo was best known for photographing celebrities and for a series of covers for *Cosmopolitan* magazine. He also took the famous nude centrefold of Burt Reynolds for *Cosmo*. We worked together on several *Cosmo* covers and he was both creative and professional. *Cosmo* liked girls with generous breasts, and mine were pretty small, so they did everything they could to make them look bigger, taping them up and stuffing my dresses! In one of the shots Francesco took, you could see my nipple. It was accidental, but they used it on the cover – it was the first women's magazine cover to reveal a nipple and caused a sensation.

Scavullo always used very beautiful lighting. He also used a make-up artist called Way Bandy, the former make-up director at Charles of the Ritz who became the world's top make-up man. He had a way of creating a very glowing look that was incredibly flattering. After Way died, rumours spread that he had mixed his foundation using his own sperm. Those of us who had worked with him – and Way had made up just about every celebrity in his day – were horrified.

Far left: The controversial cover for Cosmopolitan, June 1976. **Left:** The July 1975 issue of Cosmopolitan which the transvestite Divine later did a take-off in Andy Warhol's Interview magazine. Everyone thought I'd be offended, but I took it as a compliment! **Opposite:** Although I very rarely posed topless, I made an exception for Scavullo, as I knew he would produce a beautiful image.

Richard Avedon

Richard Avedon was a fantastic photographer who took very intimate and focused shots. He had assistants with hand-held lights so the lighting was constantly moving around you and you were free to pose in any direction. Other photographers had fixed lights on stands and you had to stay looking in one direction, but Avedon created a moving feast of light and you were free to do whatever you wanted, which was very liberating.

Opposite: Jerry Hall, dress by Gres, New York, June 7, 1979.

Horst

Horst was a German-American photographer who had taken some extraordinary photos of celebrities as far back as the thirties. When I worked with him he was in his seventies and working for American *Vogue*. His style was very arty and surrealist, I thought it was beautiful and I did quite a lot of work with him. Horst liked natural light and tungsten light; he was an old-time photographer who took very stylised black-and-white, graphic photographs. He was a charming man who was polite and thoughtful, entertaining and very knowledgeable. He loved to use a classical setting and one of my favourite photographic sessions with him was at the Rodin museum in Paris, where he pictured me alongside the stunning marble sculptures.

Arthur Elgort

Arthur Elgort was an American photographer who was a master of the use of natural light. He'd find empty buildings with sunlight coming in through doors and windows and use them as his sets. He loved sunlight streaming in through dirty windows. He didn't tell you what to do, he'd just show you the light and let you go and then snap away while you moved about. I enjoyed that – so few people use natural light and I love it – studio light is so flat in comparison. You had to move into the best possible light, so I did crazy things like climbing up a door frame in my bare feet to reach a beam. We took these pictures in Italy. Elgort never worked in England because the natural light there was just too unreliable. We worked together several times, whenever he asked for me I said yes, because I thought, 'How exciting, I get to play in the light'.

Left: Bending down to catch the light in a shot that is reminiscent of Marilyn Monroe. **Opposite:** Climbing the door frame to get to the last few rays on the same shoot. Using natural light meant that you had a very small window of opportunity to get the shot right, making flexibility key!

Gunter Sachs

Gunter was a famous photographer who was also an economist, a mathematician and an industrialist. He had been married to Brigitte Bardot and had quite a reputation as a ladies' man, but when I went to stay with him and his wife Mirja in Saint-Tropez I found a polite, charming guy. His wife was lovely, they had little children and it was all very normal. I was booked to do a shoot with him but I wouldn't go topless, so all the other girls in the photo are topless, but I've got my hands and hair covering myself. He took the shot in his house on the beach where he had a giant chessboard made out of stones.

Every photographer wanted you to do topless shots, it was a constant battle. Most of the time I said no. My mother had warned me not to do nude shots, but I wasn't just being modest – in those days if you were working for *Vogue*, which was the pinnacle of every model's career, they wouldn't work with you if you had pictures in *Playboy*. High fashion and soft porn just didn't mix, so I was always careful.

Hiro

Hiro was a great artist and a lovely man who had started out as Avedon's assistant and we worked together a lot along with the Japanese hairdresser Suga, who always worked with him.

Everything about the way Hiro worked reflected his Japanese culture. His studio was incredibly organised and minimalist, and his work was very technical and beautifully crafted. His assistants didn't have anything to do but hand him something because he knew all the technicalities and he prepared it all himself. He had a lovely personality; sweet, gentle and very giggly. I'm surprised he's not more celebrated as he took such wonderful pictures – elegant, clean, with startling colour and often with unexpected elements. We went to the Caribbean island of St. Martin to do a campaign for the Japanese designer Hanae Mori, where Hiro took this incredible photo of me, using a camera lens that NASA had developed. It was a huge close-up of my head, as I lay on the sand by the sea, looking like a giant sculpture from Easter Island. There was no retouching then, and only someone of 18 could get away with having their pores magnified like that! It was later used as a poster and in a calendar.

Bill King

Bill was pretty mad. He always wanted high energy and lots of action on his shoots, and he used to have wind machines and an assistant with a plastic water spray. He'd put on two wind machines and spritz you and shout 'jump, jump, more, more, more'. It was exhausting – you really had to be in top shape with him. Because of his style there was a kind of looniness in his pictures. You didn't always look that great because you'd be kind of leaping across the page. His look was all about energy and movement. He was fun, quite wild, a bit of a party boy. I enjoyed working with him and he booked me a lot, we had a great time together. He loved gossiping, just like Scavullo.

Bill persuaded me to do a shot which later became famous; I was topless, galloping on a horse. Now when I look at it I can't believe I agreed to do it – I hardly ever did topless shots, and it wasn't exactly safe – but he had so much energy and vitality and enthusiasm a way of getting you to do just about anything. And I have always loved riding, so I guess that helped.

Right: Very much of its time, this advert for 'SuperSuede' showcases Bill's frenetic, energetic style. **Opposite:** A shoot I did with Cheryl Tiegs and others for American Bazaar. **Above:** Bill looking very happy to be surrounded by a collection of beauties including Rene Russo, Iman, Carol Alt, Kimberley Stewart and me, of course. **Following pages:** American Bazaar, 1975.

BILL KING

THE FUN OF FITNESS!

Without the kind of body that can swing it, the slim, shape-revealing clothes you're going to see throughout this issue aren't going to mean a thing this summer. So before we go any further, we're starting where all health, beauty, and fashion begins—with fitness. On these 8 pages, a look at sports that will rev-up your body and exhilarate your mind . . . great exercise, great fun —with tips from medical experts on how to make each sport very special for you!

ACTION SPORTS

"Riding develops your sense of confidence and mastery—an asset in any challenging sport."

Willibald Nagler, M.D.

No question about it: Riding is an excellent body-toner and conditioner. You build endurance and stretch muscles by manipulating taut reins and resisting, yet controlling, the animal. Inner thighs, calves, upper arms, back and waist all benefit. . . . The new body-consciousness means doing something special for skin, too—Elizabeth Arden Body Basics is a 7-part regime of gentle cleansing, pore-tightening, toning, and moisturizing. Yellow ciré pants by Victorio De Marino for AIX. Hair and makeup on these 8 pages by Mark Sephton. Horse from Brighton Riding Stable.

See Fashion Guide for details, next to last page.

A Chilean Adventure

Neiman Marcus was the fashionable Texan store my mother and sisters and I had loved when I was very young. In those days we couldn't afford to buy anything from there, we just loved to look, so it was exciting to be asked to do a photo shoot for them. They flew me and five other models to a ski resort in Portillo, Chile, to do a shoot in the snowy mountains for their fur and diamond collections. We had six bodyguards with us, just to watch the jewels!

Just after we arrived, our resort was completely covered in deep snow; no cars could get in or out. We ended up being stuck there for three weeks, and they had to ration the food. It was a natural disaster – I know that because that was the wording the clients used as their excuse for not paying us models for the three weeks we were out of work.

While we were waiting, I decided, or was coaxed by the cute ski instructor, into taking advantage of this extra time to learn to ski. One day I went out on my own and fell into a hole and I couldn't get out. I had fallen in bottom first with my skis up in the air, and lay there like a tortoise on its back. It was freezing and I was stuck squirming for most of the day, yelling at the top of my lungs. It was getting dark and I had almost lost my voice when a soldier came up and pulled me out. I really had begun to believe that I would die that day, I was so happy to be rescued.

We models were finally airlifted out by army helicopter and we spent a day in military camp. The soldiers couldn't stop looking at us, they kept getting into trouble with their sergeants.

An Eye-opening Trip to India

During this time I went on a three-week trip to India with *Vogue Patterns* and photographer Steve Horn. We did some enchanting photos but the dresses were pretty awful! I was happy to do it, because my mother used to make us dresses from *Vogue Patterns*, before she discovered the Frederick's of Hollywood catalogue. The dresses we took to India were very simple, which is why they put them in exotic locations, to make them look glamorous.

For one shot, Steve made me climb up onto the edge of a building and hang on. I really could have killed myself – we sometimes had to do crazy things while modelling.

We travelled around India by train and I remember breakfast was made by a guy wearing what looked like a rag diaper, squatting down scrambling eggs over a little fire. Those Indian trains were pretty primitive. We took about 30 trunks of clothes and had porters to carry them around. Everywhere we went we saw examples of extreme poverty. I'd never seen anything like it before, and it was a shock.

It was in India that I took up yoga for the first time. I've done it ever since; I even made a yogacise video back in the eighties. I also tried vegetarianism in India, but after three days spent meditating and having a strange out of body experience I knew it just wasn't for me – I'm Texan and I need my steak.

Above & Opposite: Antonio posing as the photographer in these wonderfully stylised shots from our Jamaican trip for English Vogue.

To Jamaica with Norman Parkinson

Norman Parkinson was an old-style gentleman photographer and I adored him. He had one of those old fashioned plate cameras in which the shutter is held open for a few minutes while it absorbs the light. In that way it records a huge amount of movement. I worked with him many times, but one of my favourite shoots was the one we did in Jamaica with Antonio and stylist Grace Coddington, for English *Vogue*. I had invited Antonio along for the trip and it was Grace's idea to include him in the photographs. Parks used his special technique to photograph me and Antonio in a waterfall, with the water flowing behind us, so that the movement of the water was captured in a unique way. I had to stand in front of the waterfall for several minutes, but amazingly only my feet got wet!

We had great fun on that shoot. Antonio and I were such great friends and Grace and Parks were brilliant – we had some wonderful dinners in the evenings. Grace really was a genius artistically. I think she admired Antonio's work and wanted to do something with him, so she was delighted when I brought him along. Parks was quite old at that point, in his seventies. He hadn't really been considered a fashionable photographer until Grace revitalised his career by using him for *Vogue*.

Below: I love this 'wedding' shot. Everything about Antonio's pose is so stylised, even his hands. **Opposite:** Michael Jackson may have trademarked the white glove routine later, but here's proof that Antonio got there first!

The Jamaican shoot was a fusion of brilliant people. Grace has a very pictorial eye, Antonio contributed a lot of ideas and Parks' photography was inspired. It was on that trip that we did what became known as the blue series, with the blue bikini and swimming cap and gold Manolo Blahnik shoes. That resulted in my first English *Vogue* cover and 22 pages in the magazine. And it was these images which were spotted by Bryan Ferry, the lead singer of Roxy Music, who rang and asked me to appear on his next album cover.

4

BRYAN FERRY

That album cover, the glamour couple and getting engaged

I flew to London to shoot the cover of Bryan Ferry's album *Siren* in the summer of 1975. I was looking forward to meeting him – at the time he was at the height of his fame. I loved his music and thought he had the most beautiful voice, heartbreakingly touching and sexy. His band, Roxy Music, wore camp clothes, uniforms and eye-liner. They'd invented a great look – very art-house, with a mixture of rock and an element of European elegance thrown in.

After he'd collected me from the airport in his Daimler, Bryan dropped me off at the Portobello Hotel. I had a nap and that night he picked me up to take me out to dinner. This time he drove us in a black Jaguar with leather seats. When he shifted gears, his hand almost brushed my knees; there was a lot of chemistry going on between us. We had dinner with Anthony Price, a very talented clothes designer who had come up with the concepts for all Roxy Music's album covers and was working on *Siren*.

The two of them were both witty and charming and made me laugh. I was excited about the photos and Bryan seemed shy and gorgeous. He was incredibly classy and beautifully dressed and his black hair was slicked back, with just one lock that fell forwards over his eye. I was dazzled by his glamour.

That evening Bryan dropped me back at my hotel and the next morning he came to collect me for our trip to do the shoot in Wales. Anthony came with us and on the way they explained that I would be dressed as a siren, from Greek mythology, and painted blue all over. I was a bit apprehensive about that, but figured I'd just go with it and hope it worked.

It did, and though it was one of the most uncomfortable shoots I've ever done, it looked great and the album was a big success. We travelled back to London the next evening and Bryan invited me to stay in his house until I went back to New York.

During the couple of days I spent with him, Bryan and I fell for one another. I was 19 and he was 30 and we both felt we'd found what we were looking for in someone else. We laughed a lot, talked over wonderful dinners, and promised to stay in touch.

After I flew back to New York Bryan phoned me every day and I mooned around playing his albums. I loved his version of John Lennon's *Jealous Guy*.

As soon as he could get away, Bryan came to New York to visit me for a few days. I spent most of the time with him at The Carlyle; the most elegant hotel in New York. We went to a party that his record company, Atlantic Records, was giving. The Manhattan Transfer were playing there and we sat at a table with Ahmet Ertegun, the founder and chairman of Atlantic Records, and Earl McGrath who was vice president of Atlantic. I adored them both and they were so much fun; we laughed all night like old friends, but I noticed that Bryan seemed a little annoyed. It was the first time I realised that Bryan could be quite a jealous guy himself. But it didn't seem important at the time, we were young, happy and in love.

That week we also had dinner with my surrogate parents and agents, Eileen and Jerry Ford. They thought Bryan was charming but were slightly annoyed that he lived in London and might be luring me away. We also had dinner with Alvenia and my gang of girlfriends. Bryan charmed them all and passed the boyfriend inspection on all fronts.

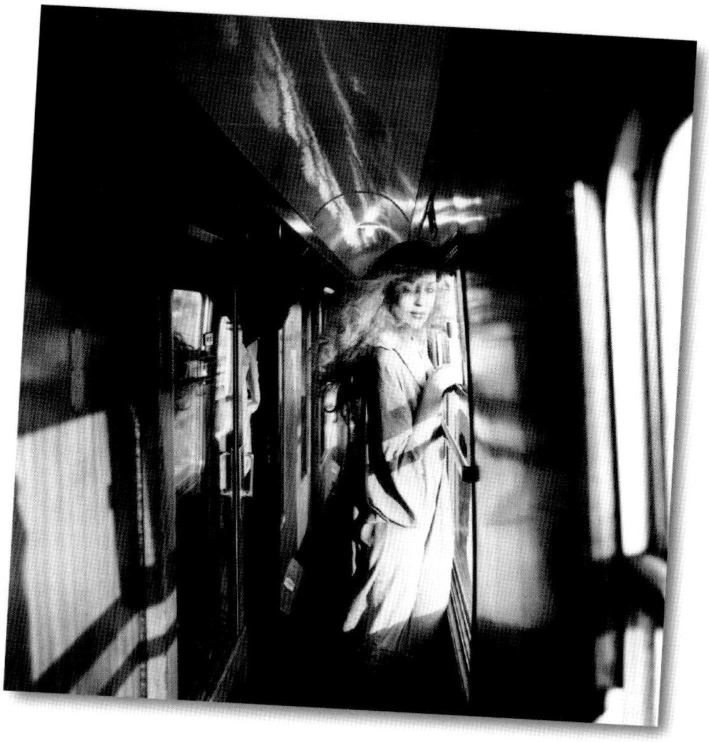

On the train to Wales for the Siren cover shoot.

When Bryan flew back to London, I promised that I would come and visit him a few weeks later, which I did. I combined it with a photo shoot for English *Vogue* and this time I stayed at Bryan's house in Ladbroke Grove. I was working during the day, but the nights were spent with Bryan. We fell into an easy intimacy, as if we had known each other longer than we had. We had a wonderful week together which neither of us wanted to end, but I had to get back to New York. I had bookings with Richard Avedon for American *Vogue* and some big-paying commercials and advertising campaigns that I couldn't cancel.

Bryan invited me to come back a few weeks later to spend Christmas with him and then go on holiday to Mustique in the southern Caribbean for a month. I knew my booker, Marion at Ford Models, would not be pleased, but living so far away from each other we had to spend some real time together to see if our relationship could work on a long-term basis.

So a few weeks later I returned to London for a traditional English Christmas with all the trimmings, including crackers from Fortnum and Mason containing little silver shoehorns and cufflinks and tiny hand mirrors for your purse. We had some of Bryan's friends over – musicians and old school friends – and then on Boxing Day we flew to Mustique where we spent an idyllic four weeks and at the end of it Bryan proposed and we got engaged. I was stunned when he proposed because we hadn't been together that long. But I was thrilled too.

Soon after that I moved to London to live with Bryan. I worked mostly for English *Vogue*, and I went on tour with Bryan to Manchester to promote *Siren*. I met Bryan's family who were adorable and so kind to me. They were very proud of Bryan. He had bought them a new house and they were so happy about it. His father had been a coal miner and they were quite poor when Bryan was little.

Siren was a huge success, so Bryan was away on tour a lot and I couldn't always go with

On stage at Bottom Line with Roxy Music

him because I was working too. So while he was away I started to read. I went through his library and then started buying books by the bagful and bringing them home. I was getting the education that I had missed by not going to university. I loved reading about Greek mythology and was fascinated by archetypal images and stories of brave and powerful women. I often set out to portray these powerful women in the photo shoots I did.

Life with Bryan settled into a pattern. A lot of the time we lived quietly – I would shop and cook when I got home and the two of us would eat together. We had some happy times, but I was beginning to feel a sense of disquiet. Bryan wanted to be an English gentleman. He dressed in fine clothes, knew about art and antiques and shopped in Fortnum and Mason. And he wanted me to be a gentleman's wife, in tweeds and pearls and sipping afternoon tea. Actually I quite liked that part; I got in the habit of having afternoon tea every day. But while I had a very ladylike side, which had been encouraged by my mother, I also had a wild side. I didn't drink much at all, but I loved to party and dance and have fun. But every time I did, Bryan seemed to disapprove.

Back in Texas I had been a champion leg-wrestler and sometimes I told people about it, and once I even gave a demonstration, accompanied by a lot of hootin' and hollerin'. Bryan was embarrassed and told me to stop, and I ended up in tears.

Although we were engaged, Bryan wouldn't commit to setting a date for our wedding. He was becoming more distant; he would often sit staring into the distance, deep in thought, for hours on end.

Of course we didn't spend all our time alone. We were good friends with David Bailey and his model wife Marie Helvin, and with Anthony Price and the rest of Bryan's band. I would invite people over and try and give dinner parties and have some fun. But often Bryan would either not join us for dinner or be rude and cold to my friends, especially if they were straight men.

After the tour was over, late in 1976, Bryan decided to record a solo album. He had done a lot of cover songs and was trying to write some songs of his own. He worked in the basement with a keyboard and he became very moody and bad-tempered. It was a cold winter and often dark and rainy and I felt very alone. I was still only 20 and I missed the sun, my friends and my sisters.

I used to tell Bryan about my twin Terry and the pact we'd made as kids – 'twins forever stick together'. We'd put it at the end of our letters. Bryan wrote a song, *Let's Stick Together*, which he released on an album of the same name and then as a single. Both the album and the single were hits and I got to sing along on the video for the song. I even did a live performance with him, in New York at a small club called the Bottom Line. I painted myself with gold dust and I had on a leopard-skin swimsuit with a long tail at the back. I came out hollerin' Texas-style and swung the tail around; I really hammed it up. Antonio came to watch us, and so did Andy Warhol and Eileen and Jerry Ford and they all shouted 'bring back Jerry' once I had finished, which made Bryan very uncomfortable.

While we were in the States we went to Texas to introduce Bryan to my family. My mother thought Bryan was handsome and my father loved telling him war stories. But as we sat down to eat, a big cockroach crawled across the dining room floor. In Texas we have a lot of creatures around, it's no big deal to us, so my father put his foot out and smashed the cockroach. Bryan looked horrified and and just picked at the delicious home cooked feast that we girls had worked so hard to prepare. Unsurprisingly, my sisters didn't really care much for Bryan after that.

Back in London The Rolling Stones came to town and we went to see their show. I was a big Stones fan and loved their music and I was blown away by Mick Jagger's performance. He seemed to jump so high he could almost fly and the audience were on their feet dancing like crazy. After the show we were invited back to Mick's hotel room at the Ritz. There were half a dozen people there and Mick was wearing a red silk dressing gown. He was friendly to us both and asked us to dinner.

Bryan was flattered by Mick's attention, but he could also see that Mick was smitten with me. It couldn't have been nice for him. At the end of the evening, Mick brushed his leg next to mine. I felt an electric jolt!

We'd been together for a year and a half when Bryan set off on a world tour. He said that I couldn't come and asked me if I could find somewhere to stay as he had just sold his London house to John Cleese. John had been over to see the house and had tripped over a leather stool in the sitting room, just like his character in Fawlty Towers.

When Bryan left me behind that spring, I felt my dreams of happiness fade away. I had spent the last of my teenage years with him. I'm sure I was often loud and rowdy, that I was not quite polished and sometimes acted as a bit of a loose cannon. I had been his Pygmalion, he had tried to smooth out the rough edges and I had sometimes resented it, though I had tried hard to make him happy.

With nowhere to live in London, I decided to go and stay with my sister Cyndy in New York, and catch up with friends.

Shooting Roxy Music's *Siren* Cover

The day after I arrived in England, Bryan and I travelled by train down to Wales to do the cover shoot for his new album *Siren*. Anthony Price and the photographer Graham Hughes travelled down with us, and we all stayed in a little seaside hotel. The four of us had dinner, trading tales and stories with lots of laughter. After dinner I went to bed and pin-curled my hair, ready for the following day's shoot. I was all tucked up in bed in my nightie when Bryan knocked on my door. I opened it and peered round it at him and he asked if he could come in for a minute. I let him in but got back under the covers as I felt a bit embarrassed. He sat on a chair beside the bed and asked if my room was alright. I said yes, wondering how silly I looked in my hair curlers. Bryan leaned over me and kissed me on the lips, said goodnight and left. His kiss was delicious! I slept so well that night.

The next day we started very early. I was meant to be a mystical siren who lures men onto the rocks, so Anthony had made me a blue mermaid outfit. He also painted my entire body blue and gave me long blue false nails! The pin-curling had left my hair a waist-length mass of wiry curls.

Left: Fooling around with Bryan on the train to Wales, snapped by the shoot photographer Graham Hughes. The chemistry between the pair of us really was electric.

Left: Applying the final touches before heading onto the shoot, with Bryan and Anthony looking on. **Below:** A few shots of Bryan and I taken while Anthony was putting the final touches to the mermaid outfit he had designed for me. Sadly this amazing costume is barely visible in the final shot.

We did the *Siren* shoot on a hot summer day and the volcanic rocks that I was lying on were very uncomfortable. Bryan held an umbrella over my head during the breaks, to stop the body paint melting. But the costume had been glued together and the glue melted and stuck to me! Then, just when we were ready to shoot, some kids went past in a yellow rubber raft and we all shouted 'get out of the picture!' In the end the shot took all day and by the time we got back to the hotel we didn't have long before we needed to catch our train back to London. Anthony had to help scrub off the blue paint and glue off my body while I stood in the bath and Bryan watched, leaning against the door with a cigarette, laughing, because the paint wouldn't come off.

We ran out of time, so they wrapped me in towels, still covered in greasy blue paint and still wearing my blue nails and long false eyelashes. By that time it was pouring with rain and I was dripping blue paint everywhere. I tried to get cleaned up on the train, but it still wouldn't come off, so when we got to London Bryan asked me to come to his house for a hot bath. I did, and when I was finally clean and wrapped in a towelling robe he invited me to stay the night in his guest room. That was the night our romance began. He took me out to dinner and we discovered that we loved a lot of the same things, like Elvis, and Hitchcock movies. I stayed with him for a couple of days before heading back to New York, but we promised to keep in touch.

Left: Taking a break between shots. Bryan was given the job of covering me with the umbrella because it was so hot and the glue that was holding my costume together was melting, but whenever I turned around I'd find he had it over himself, not me!

Left: One of the shots that was considered for the album cover.
Above: The finished cover. Although it was an extremely difficult shoot because of the location and the hot weather, I think the final result was well worth it. I love the positioning of my arms, it really looks as though I am clambering out of the sea and onto the rocks.

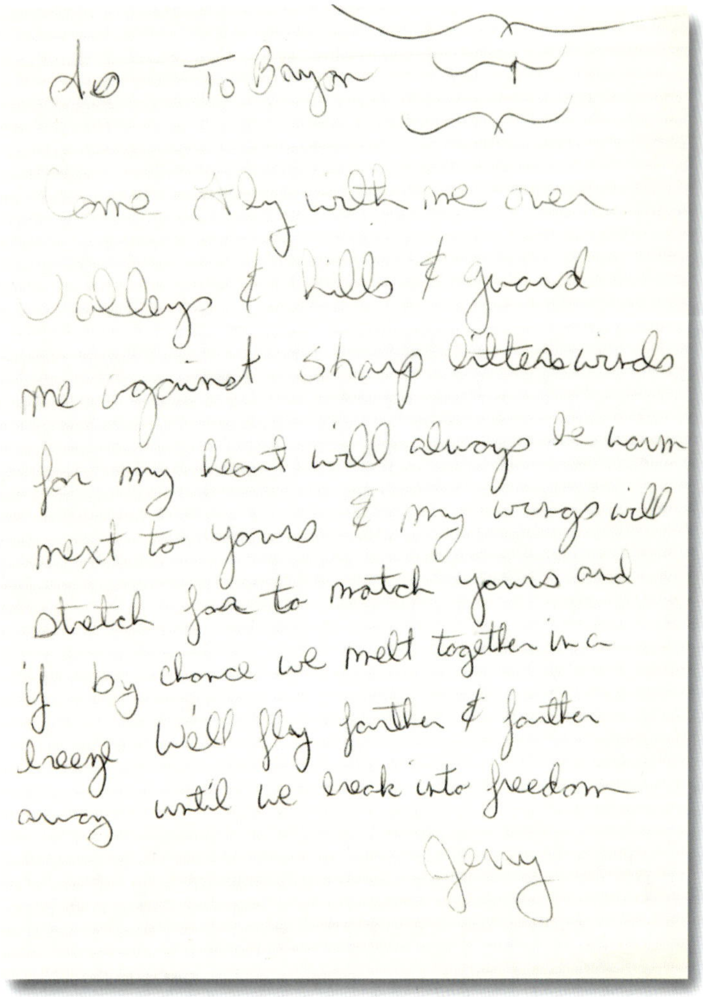

do To Bryan

Come fly with me over
valleys & hills & guard
me against sharp bitter winds
for my heart will always be warm
next to yours & my wings will
stretch far to match yours and
if by chance we melt together in a
breeze we'll fly farther & farther
away until we break into freedom

Jerry

Left: This note to Bryan was inspired by the novella Jonathan Livingston Seagull. Only when you're 19 do you write a love note like that. Everything feels perfect, you're in love.

A Fairytale Romance in Mustique

On Boxing Day 1975 Bryan and I flew off to Mustique to spend a month together. We needed time away from our busy schedules, to get to know one another and find out whether we really wanted to be together. We stayed in a gorgeous six-bedroom villa called the Gingerbread House. It had been designed by Oliver Messel and belonged to Colin Tennant, who had bought the island and turned it into a private luxury retreat. We shared the house with Bryan's friend Charles Benson, the racing tipster for the *Daily Express* who was known as 'the Scout', and his fiancée Carolyn. They were both great fun to be with. Bryan and I went snorkelling and boating and acted like the kids we were. We had such a heavenly time together and fell so in love that by the end of the month he had asked me to marry him and I had said yes. He gave me a beautiful flower-shaped ruby and diamond engagement ring. I was so in love, I believed my life was turning out to be happier than I had ever hoped for.

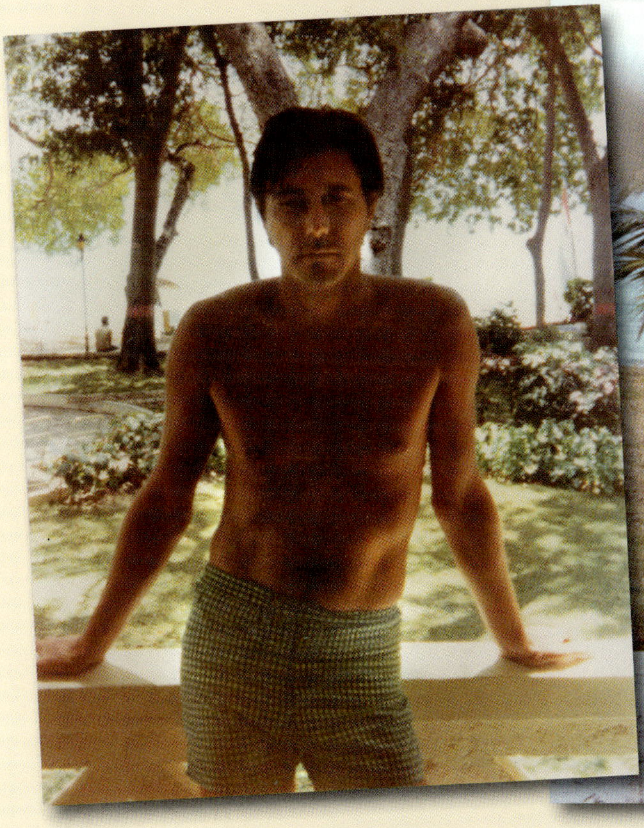

Left: Snaps from our time in Mustique. I can't quite believe how young I look in these!

Left: Photographed by Brian Aris and looking every bit the glamorous couple. **Opposite:** Bryan and I did a lot of photoshoots together. This Men in Vogue cover, shot by David Bailey, is one of my favourites.

The Perfect Couple?

Siren, the album Bryan had made with Roxy Music with me on the cover, came out in late 1975 and was a huge hit – it's still in the top 500 albums of all time – and two singles from it were also chart hits. In 1976, when I moved to England to be with Bryan, he was hugely popular and I was one of the world's most successful models. We were seen as a perfect couple, and we did a lot of photos and interviews for the press as publicity for his record and tour. Everywhere we went we were snapped by the paparazzi. Bryan was always torn between wanting the exposure and wanting to keep our life together private. I felt that once he had arrived and was a success, he found it hollow and empty; he'd had more fun trying to get there.

MEN
IN VOGUE

Lady of the Manor

Bryan had such a lovely, funny, playful side; but after a year together I was seeing less and less of the Bryan that I had fallen in love with. He dreamed of being an aristocratic man of leisure, swanning around his country estate in tweeds and handmade shoes. And he became very critical of me. He wanted me to dress like Kim Novak in Vertigo – in a grey suit, with pearls around my neck and my hair in a French twist. When the two of us were alone he would spend hours staring off into space and when we went to dinner he wouldn't let me talk. He became jealous and started going through my handbag and finding cards or telephone numbers on bits of paper that I'd been given at parties, then questioning me about them. I started to spend a lot of time in my dressing room crying. It was a lonely time, I felt the dreams I'd had about our life together were crumbling.

Opposite: Although it looks very staged and styled, this is actually an ordinary photo! The outfit I'm in is very much the look which Bryan liked. Once we were engaged he always wanted me to wear grey suits and country tweeds.

5

LONDON CALLING

Living in London, working with English Vogue

All my friends in New York thought I was crazy when I moved to London to be with Bryan. Eileen Ford was devastated and begged me not to go. But besides being in love, I actually thought it was better for me creatively. I had been doing such tremendous photographs with English *Vogue* and I wanted to do more. Grace Coddington, the stylist there was a creative genius and they had some hugely talented photographers – Norman Parkinson, David Bailey and Terence Donovan. We were doing really beautiful pictures – lasting iconic images I felt very proud of. It was a more creative, less commercial work environment than in the States. It was the end of the golden era of Hollywood glamour goddesses and also a time of women's liberation and sexual liberation. People were looking for strong new women role models and fashion was reflecting that need.

In London no-one wanted to cut my hair, I was set free creatively and it was such a relief and fun too. I joined the London-based agency, Models One, run by Jose Fonseca and Dick Kreis. They were great agents and we became best friends.

London was a great place to be. In the sixties, London had been the most swinging place in the world, and in the seventies, when I arrived, it was still a buzzing place full of clever and creative people, with Punk the big movement on the street and in the music scene. Designer Vivienne Westwood and her partner Malcolm McLaren – manager of the Sex Pistols – had a shop called Sex that I used to visit a lot. Malcolm and Vivienne worked in the shop and we met and made friends then. I loved Vivienne's style; her clothes were so different and sexy.

The Clash was a happening band then. Joe Strummer was writing great rebel songs like *I'm So Bored With The USA* and the Punk movement spread like wildfire. When you walked down the street there were young people with bright pink, green or purple hair. They stood out in all the grey drizzle. I found that hard to get used to. In New York even when it's cold it's always sunny, there's light. But in London the light goes.

Iman and me.

Work was exciting. I was doing a lot of work with Bailey, who was *the* photographer in London then. And I became very good friends with his wife Marie Helvin. She'd started modelling at about the same time as me, Antonio and I used to see her in English *Vogue* and we thought she was so beautiful. Then we met doing the collections and when I moved to London we became close because we were the only girls working there all the time. For about a year we were on alternate covers of English *Vogue* – one month Marie, the next month me, and so on. Marie and I used to work together, hang out together and go shopping together. We had similar taste in clothes – we both liked well-cut sexy and glamorous clothes and hated boring English tweeds.

Bryan and I sometimes asked people over to dinner. We loved to ask Anthony Price, the designer, who usually had a boyfriend in tow. Then there was film director John Schlesinger and his partner, and two sisters from Brazil, models Christina and Rio. We also saw a lot of designer Bruce Oldfield, Vivienne Westwood and the rest of the band members in Roxy Music. And when Norman Parkinson and his wife Wanda came over from Tobago we'd see them. It was quite a small world, really.

Out on the town with Marie Helvin.

Sometimes we'd go out to Tramp or Annabel's and bump into Michael Caine and his wife Shakira. I loved to dance, but Bryan never really did, he was quite shy. We'd eat in Langan's Brasserie, and sometimes we'd go to the legendary parties thrown by socialite Nona Summers and her husband Martin, where you'd bump into stars like Warren Beatty and Jack Nicholson.

One of the things I loved about being in England was the sense of humour. The English are like schoolboys – always playing tricks on each other or making you feel as if you're in on a secret joke. The Texans and the English have a common bond of eccentricity. They thrive on it. But they also have a straight-laced, uptight side. I have a bit of both myself, and I really enjoyed it.

It was in the summer of 1976 that I first met Mick, when Bryan and I went to see the Stones in concert in London. We all went out to dinner after the show, and after that Mick would turn up at our house. Mick was so different to Bryan, he didn't care what anyone thought and he laughed all the time. He'd be jumping around and joking and Bryan would get very edgy. I'd go into the kitchen to make tea and Mick would follow me and then Bryan would follow him. One time Mick started chasing me around the ping-pong table, trying to kiss me, and Bryan came in and chased him out.

Mick started leaving messages on the answer phone, saying 'Hi Bryan, let's go out again' and Bryan said, 'I'm never going out with him again, all he did was ogle you all night.' But I found myself thinking about Mick, and that worried me, because Bryan and I were engaged and I didn't want to think about anyone else. And then Bryan set off on his world tour and I went back to New York, feeling sad and uncertain about the future.

Left: Enjoying a glass of champagne and a chat with David and Marie.
Opposite: Marie and I were like big fish in a small pond in England during this period – we were all over the covers of every magazine. This Tatler cover, shot by Bailey, is a rare example of the pair of us on the front together.

David Bailey: A Living Legend

I first met David Bailey when I was 16 and in Paris, modelling for the Kenzo fashion show. He was there watching his wife Marie Helvin, who was already a very successful model. A couple of years later I met Bailey again when we did a job together for the *Sunday Times* newspaper. He was wickedly funny, made me laugh, and said it was great to meet 'a real broad!'

By that time I was 19 and living in London with Bryan Ferry and I got to know Bailey really well. I did a lot of work with Marie, she and I became best friends, and I spent a lot of time at their home.

Bailey and I always got on incredibly well and had lots of friends in common, so we often socialised and had dinner together. And of course we did a lot of work together too. I loved working with him because he was a true original. He had taken some of the most famous and iconic pictures of the sixties. His sharp, simple black-and-white photos of Michael Caine, Jean Shrimpton, the Beatles and the Stones captured the essence of sixties cool. And having been married to Catherine Deneuve and then Marie, he achieved a kind of pop star status of his own; he was sexy and cool as well as a great artist and he became one of the first real celebrity photographers.

Bailey is an authentic person who loves beauty in all its forms. He is now married to Catherine Dyer and they have three gorgeous children – one of whom is my godson Sasha. Bailey is a cuddly, funny and warm man who is great fun to be with. He was and is my favourite photographer, and as a friend I love him dearly.

TATLER
Twin Sept
£1.50
LET'S HAVE LUNCH!
Craig Brown on the boys who lunched with a man who waved to a guy who worked for David Puttnam
SHARE GENIUS
To him that hath: Britain's biggest perks
REAL QUICHE
doesn't beat Elizabeth David
MARIE HELVIN AND JERRY HALL
PHOTOGRAPHED BY DAVID BAILEY
It's wild! It's rich! It's heady! It's frothy! Look out, Hollywood! It's –
GUINNESSTY

F

Above: A series of images that Bailey took of Marie and me for French Vogue. I love the atmosphere of these shots, they feel as though they could have been taken in a much earlier period. We took these shots very quickly before heading for a long brasserie lunch. Modelling was so much more relaxed back then.

Opposite: These are my favourite David Bailey shots. I really like the contrast between the poses that I am striking, and those of the sculptures beneath me.

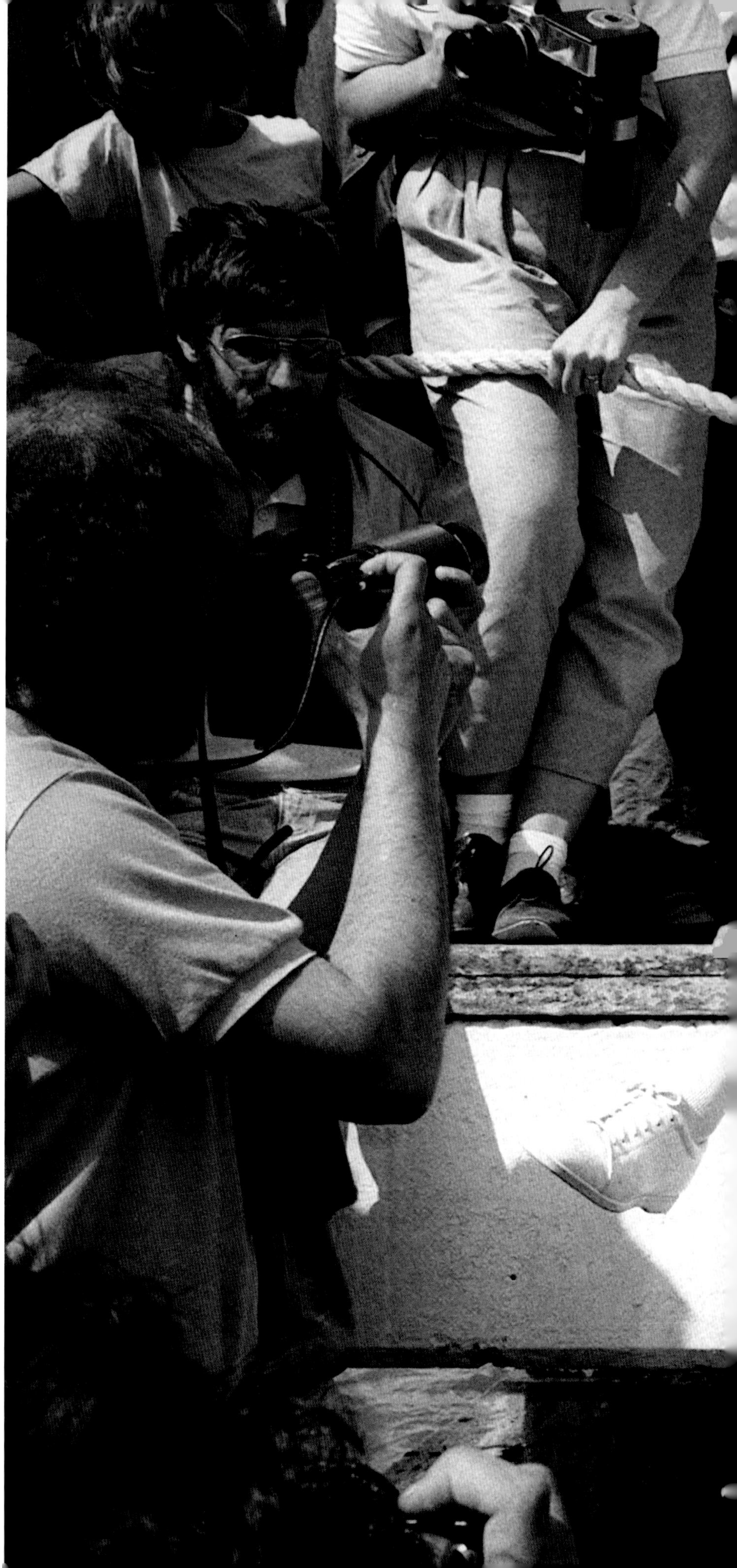

Right: While we were in the south of France we visited the Cannes Film Festival, where we met an old friend, Helmut Newton. With typical humour, Bailey photographed us together, along with the press pack that had gathered, swarming around us and snapping away.

Acting up on the Catwalk

Modelling was enormously enjoyable in the late seventies and eighties and I was very lucky to be in demand a lot. When the collections were shown I worked very hard – sometimes doing 35 catwalk shows a week, followed by 35 more the following week and the week after that. But it was a time of great creativity, excitement and innovation and I loved being a part of it.

It was such hard work that you'd lose a lot of weight during those hectic weeks. The same models would be doing all the shows and of course we got to be great friends; it was all a lot of fun. The top models then were Appolonia, Pat Cleveland, Susy Dyson, Iman, from Somalia, Kirat, who was Indian and the Brazilian model Dalma. In those days there were no paparazzi photographers or TV cameras backstage, so all the girls would relax and chat. Nowadays backstage is always full of press, there's one interview after another with full-on cameras, you don't have a moment away. The same photographers and magazine editors would be at each show too, and we'd all go out and eat every evening after the shows – pasta in Italy, sushi in Japan. Nowadays the shows are held in huge places and are packed with hundreds of fashion students, freelancers and so on. Back then everything was smaller and more intimate.

There's a skill to catwalk modelling, a haughtiness you have to convey. You have to look super-cool, so that everyone wants what you're wearing, and to be as cool as you. You have to get in character, just as much as when you're acting. But that's where the similarity ends, because in acting you have to show the character's flaws, their dark side, while in modelling you're trying to be graceful, to project a visual.

Left: I love the rush of runway modelling. A typical show can involve changing anything up to eight times, so backstage can get pretty chaotic, with everyone rushing around, getting made up, dressed and ready.

To Russia with Parks

English *Vogue* asked me to go to Russia with Norman Parkinson and Grace Coddington. Although his manners were impeccable, Parks was quite a taskmaster. In the thirties he had done the most stunning photographs of an athletic model, in a white swimsuit and turban, diving off a cliff into the water, and now we wanted to develop the theme. We'd already done the blue shoot in Jamaica in which I wore a blue swimsuit and cap and the plan was to do a red series in Russia, as a continuation of those athletic iconic images of strong powerful women.

In Russia we were accompanied by state guides telling us what to do and where we could and could not photograph. They wanted to show the New Russia and Parks used all the obstacles they put in our way to his advantage. He had me climbing up oil rigs waving big red flags and posing on a styrofoam plinth, which we carried everywhere we went. When I was posing on it in the Dead Sea in a red swimsuit the passers-by looked shocked at my lack of modesty. The women there wore flowered headscarves and long dresses, and the men averted their eyes. When we were leaving our Russian guides said they would develop the film in Russia and send it to us. Parks was worried that they would edit it, so he asked me to smuggle it out in my pants. He was very persuasive, so eventually I agreed. I was so nervous! They checked everything and confiscated my Bryan Ferry cassettes, but thankfully they didn't look in my pants. Growing up in Texas we had often had drills to practice in the event of a nuclear war with the Russians. We had to hide under our desks - as if that would protect us. But because of that I was paranoid the whole time. I was so relieved to get back to London I kissed the tarmac!

Above: Atop a statue in my red swimsuit. These photos referenced the pictures Parks had taken of me in Jamaica, though the location could not have been more different.
Opposite: A Texan girl waving the Soviet flag right in the middle of the Cold War. I wonder what Mama made of this at the time?

ТВОЙ ВКЛА
В ДЕВЯТУ
ПЯТИЛЕТ

Versailles in *Vogue*

Another memorable shoot for English *Vogue* was in Versailles, the seventeenth century French palace. Once again Norman Parkinson, Grace Coddington and I worked together, this time in the chambers of the legendary French Queen, Marie Antoinette, who was married at 14 to Louis XV1 and beheaded at the tender age of 37, during the French revolution.

Parks photographed me in her bedroom and rather than think about what had happened to her, I trusted my intuition to tell me what to do. Modelling is very intuitive, it's about going with your instinct, the feel of the fabric and the period of the clothes. When the camera was clicking I would empty my mind and use only the non-thinking part of my brain, completely absorbed in what I was doing. In the same way art and poetry are about feeling, so is modelling.

Opposite: Dancing around in front of the Palace of Versailles' gilded finery. **Right:** Striking a reflective pose on Marie Antoinette's bed.

In the royal chambers I was definitely aware of the presence of Marie Antoinette as I moved around; there was a real feeling of sadness in the place.

I wore a draped red dress which I felt was quite ugly, and looked better draped as I leaned forward, so that's how I showed it. Your job as a model is to make the dress look as good as possible, so I always did a lot of experimenting in front of a mirror before going on set, to see which way the dress was going to look most interesting, because in the end fashion is about selling the dresses. And I always tried to make sure that I was in the right pose the moment the camera flash went off, with my hair and the dress just right.

Following pages: I love this picture, taken by Norman Parkinson in the Bois de Boulogne for English Vogue. I knew Iman well, and we made a great couple of *femmes fatales*.

Left: Arm in arm, out and about and having fun in front of the cameras. Don't we look young?

6

MEETING MICK JAGGER

Falling for the greatest rock star in the world

Back in New York, I threw myself into work. Bryan was touring Japan and Australia for several months and he wrote me a letter saying it was too expensive to call. Then I heard from a hairdresser at work that Bryan was having an affair with a model in Japan.

One day I was working with another hairdresser Ara Gallant, who was doing my hair for a photo which Francesco Scavullo wanted to include in a book called *Scavullo on Beauty*. Ara did sensational, wild hair and was very much in demand. He invited me to a dinner party with the aristocratic English model Penelope Tree, and I found myself sitting between Mick and Warren Beatty, both of whom were fighting for my attention.

Mick was wearing a white silk suit and a red silk shirt. He made me laugh all night. After dinner we went to some live music clubs and we ended up at the Bottom Line, watching Lou Reed perform and then going on to Studio 54, the happening place. It was a wonderful evening – May 21, 1977 – the day Mick and I got together. We would celebrate that day for the next 23 years. Mick was gentle, charming, funny and fascinating. I loved the way he didn't seem to care a hoot what people thought of him. He was confident and cool and always in control.

At the end of the evening he dropped off Ara and another friend first. When we stopped I went to say goodbye and then realised we weren't at my place. Mick said it was his house and to please come in for a cup of tea. I did, and from that moment on, Mick laid siege to me. He started sending me flowers and getting me invited to dinners where he would be seated next to me. And I was flattered. He was witty and bright and utterly persistent.

I started an affair with him, on the condition that it would be over at the end of the summer when Bryan came back. I told Mick that I couldn't see him every day, only every other day. It was a futile attempt to protect my heart, because I was falling in love with him.

Mick had told me that he took LSD every day for a year in the sixties. The Stones thought it was mind expanding. He also admitted that he was smoking heroin. I was shocked and disgusted, I told him I couldn't see him if he took drugs. I said, 'go away and don't come back until you're straight'. He did get straight; he had amazing willpower.

My father had been ill for a long time with lymphoma. I had flown down to Dallas a few weeks before and seen him in hospital. I hardly recognised him. The powerful, menacing man that I had grown up fearing had been replaced by a frail, repentant one. He had been ravaged by cancer, but he was beaming at me and full of pride. My mother and all my sisters were there and I felt we made a kind of peace. When he died I was surprised by how upset I was. I sent a telegram to Bryan begging him to call me, but he just sent back a telegram with his condolences and I felt very hurt. I turned to Mick, who was supportive and consoling. While most men aren't very good at feelings, Mick had a talent for it.

Mick was writing songs for the album *Some Girls*. I met Ronnie Wood, who was staying at Mick's house, and I had dinner one night with Mick, Keith Richards and Ronnie when they were recording, but mostly Mick and I kept a very low profile. We managed to stay out of the papers, and carried on discreetly seeing each other for the rest of the summer.

This T-shirt says it all.

For my twenty-first birthday in July, Mick gave me an exquisite pair of diamond hoop antique earrings. Then summer ended and we said a tearful goodbye. Bryan was due back the next day and I was to move into the Carlyle Hotel with him for a few days before we went on to a house Bryan had rented in Los Angeles for six months. I felt confused and full of mixed feelings.

When Bryan arrived back I was happy to see him. He gave me a beautiful emerald bracelet that said, 'Remember', for the birthday he had missed. I hoped I could forget about Mick and make a fresh start with Bryan. We flew to Los Angeles and moved into a little adobe house in Bel Air.

In Los Angeles Bryan and I did a lot of socialising and I was terrified that he would find out what I had been up to. It was 1977 and we went to Joan Collins' Bangers and Mash Party for the Queen's Silver Jubilee – Joan looking amazing in short shorts. At one party I met Paul Newman; he was so gorgeous, and James Coburn whom I had admired in *The Magnificent Seven* at the drive-in in Mesquite. It was very strange living in Hollywood; when I went grocery shopping I would see famous people and start to say 'hello' to them, thinking I knew them, but I didn't, I just recognised them.

I carried on modelling in LA, mostly for department stores like Saks, Fifth Avenue, Bullock's and Neiman Marcus. It paid well and they were excited to have me there. Bryan played a lot of tennis with Richard Price, the record producer. One night we all had dinner, together with Earl McGrath of Atlantic Records and the Stones' manager, Prince Rupert Loewenstein. When Bryan was out of the room, Rupert passed me Mick's telephone number on a piece of paper.

Mick had also been calling my sister Cyndy a lot, insisting that I phone him. So I rang him from a telephone booth at the supermarket the next day. He begged to see me again, telling me how much he missed me. I was going to Paris to do some photos with French *Vogue* and the October fashion shows, so we arranged to meet up while I was there.

In the desert in Morocco.

I felt horribly torn. I loved both Bryan and Mick. I missed Mick and thought about him a lot. I knew what we had wasn't over yet. I wanted to end it with Bryan, but the LA sunshine had cheered him up and he was being so sweet to me so I just couldn't bring myself to do it.

I went to Paris to join Mick and as soon as I saw him again I knew I wanted to be with him. After the shows we decided to go to Morocco for a holiday. I rang Bryan and said I had a modelling job. Mick and I lost our suitcase at the airport, so we bought some Moroccan gowns with hoods and some T-shirts and jogging trousers. We went to our hotel, but we were invited by the town's mayor to stay as guests at his house. We had to escape fast when our host tried to buy me from Mick, who kept joking that he'd been tempted to sell, but the mayor had only offered fifty camels for me.

We drove around in a rented car, wearing our hooded gowns, with black kohl around our eyes and listening to great music. We felt so free. We stayed in hotels where the rooms were full of sweet-scented bowls of roses and lit by candles, and we sat by the open fire while Mick played his guitar and sang to me. I loved the way Mick didn't complain and he laughed at all the mad things that kept happening.

We were having lunch at the Club Med in Agadir when I ran into a fashion editor I knew. I told her we had lost our bags and she lent us some clothes from her photo shoot – crazy matching Claude Montana leather outfits, red for Mick, white for me.

I was still phoning Bryan and telling him that I was on a modelling job. Finally he said, 'stop lying, I read about you and Mick in Morocco in the papers'. I guess the fashion team must have spilled the beans. Bryan said, 'just come home and we'll talk about it'. But I couldn't, I knew he was not the forgiving type and I was already too much in love with Mick. Bryan and I talked and cried for hours. I felt really bad for breaking off our engagement and running off the way I did. It never occurred to me to complain about the affair he had had in Japan.

Bryan took me leaving him very badly. He kept all my clothes and things and wouldn't let me have any of them back. I had left a book by the bed called *The Mists of Avalon*, about druids. Bryan wrote a beautiful album called *Avalon* that was a huge success. But he never spoke to me again.

It was the third time I had lost everything and just taken off with one suitcase. I knew I was throwing caution to the wind, but my love was so strong I couldn't do anything but follow Mick wherever he would lead me. I knew he had a reputation as a womaniser and he was still married. He hadn't been living with Bianca for over a year, but it was another complication. But I was hopeful. I thought that as I had got him to quit heroin, I could get him to give up womanising as well.

Mick and I moved in together, we rented a lovely little apartment right beside Notre Dame in Paris. Mick was to start recording the *Some Girls* album and I was back working for French *Vogue*. I would work in the day, then go back home to Mick who was sleeping. I would sleep for a few hours then we would wake up around ten at night, make love and then go out to dinner and get to the studio around midnight.

It was fun getting to know the Stones and their women and listening to this great music being created. I was fascinated to see them working together. Mick would produce some lyrics and they would start jamming. Keith would write some music and, without appearing to talk, they would just start playing all these great songs. It really did seem as if some magical alchemy was at work. Keith would always light a candle and say, 'nobody writes a song, they are just out there and you have to know how to catch them'.

I was now part of the Stones set-up; the band members, their wives, girlfriends and children and the support crew that worked and travelled with them. As Mick's girl I lived and worked alongside the band, which meant life in a constant spotlight. Wherever we went we were followed by fans and photographers. When we went on tour, we were given police escorts to our hotels, where we were protected from the thousands of fans outside by armies of security guards. If we wanted to go out we had to be taken through the hotel kitchens and sneaked into windowless vans which slipped through the back entrances. If we wanted to visit museums or art exhibitions or shops then we went early in the morning before opening time, or late at night after they closed. Life was very different to the way it had been when I was growing up, or even when I was modelling, before I got together with Mick and it took a while to get used to it. Because we were together so much the Stones 'family' became very close. When I wasn't working I hung out with the other Stones girls while the guys played and later, when we all had kids, they all played together and ended up becaming close friends.

Soon after we got together Mick and Bianca divorced. He wasn't nearly as rich as people thought, and he had to give her most of what he had. But we were free to be together.

With Mick in Mustique.

Making Magic with Mick

Mick and I seemed to work some kind of magic together at this time – everything we did was successful and we were being hailed as *the* glitterati couple. We were invited to everything, met everyone and were photographed wherever we went – it was all very heady stuff.

Perhaps it was because we were so happy. We really were head over heels in love. When I first went to Paris to be with Mick, while he recorded an album and I did the catwalk shows, we made love four times a day; at every opportunity we were ripping each other's clothes off. We never got tired or bored or disagreed. We were just so in love, becoming closer and closer, sharing our thoughts, our books, our inner fears and always laughing. He would read me the spiritual poetry of Rumi and I would read him the humorous poetry of Dorothy Parker.

We laughed together all the time. Mick had a great sense of humour, he was always joking and we both loved playing games and fooling around. I had been a leg-wrestling champion back in Texas. Bryan had disapproved and the one time he saw me leg-wrestle, at a party in Mustique where everyone was having fun, he was angry with me and told me not to do it. But Mick thought it was hilarious, he really got into leg-wrestling.

Left: Mick and I backstage at an event, shot by Norman Parkinson.

The Rock 'n' Roll Superstar

Above & Opposite: Whether strutting, singing or striking a pose Mick's stage presence has always been electric.
Following pages: Mick taking centre stage in front of thousands of fans at a performance in Soldier Field, Chicago, 1978.

Mick really was the greatest showman on earth. When he got on stage he became this incredible magnetic creature. I loved watching him perform, with his feet stomping, and his hands clapping; I couldn't take my eyes off him. He was ridiculously glamorous and when he smiled the diamond in his tooth caught the light and flashed at you. He was an athlete; every show demanded a huge amount of energy.

He was also a great songwriter. He would keep a diary and write down all his emotions. Then he would pick through his notes and work them into songs. He would also take stories from what was going on in the world and craft powerful, haunting lyrics. He had some of the same books that Bryan Ferry had used for song writing: rhyming dictionaries and the French poets Baudelaire and Rimbaud.

When it came to the band, Mick was the brains behind everything. He had incredible ambition and drive, he was the engine that kept it all going; he was the one with the foresight, who planned for the future. He was a real Leo; very clever, very ambitious and very competitive. Mick had a lot of diplomatic skills, he would always smooth out problems. He had a way of talking to people that worked, he was very firm and persuasive. He held it all together.

Up Close and Personal with the Rolling Stones

Below: Cowboy hats all round!
Opposite: Life with the Stones was often a lot of fun; it was like being part of a big family. Being on tour was like living in a bubble, and we would end up spending a lot of time together backstage.

Keith really is a pirate, but he has a big-hearted, generous, and loyal side too. He was the guts and the sage of the Stones, but it was Mick who was the mesmerising magician. They had this symbiotic relationship which meant they could construct brilliant songs in just a couple of hours. Keith and Mick are the same age and have known each other since they went to the same primary school in Kent in the early fifties. They met again as students, when Mick was at the London School of Economics and Keith was at Art College, and Mick invited Keith to join the band he was in. When that disbanded, they formed the Rolling Stones.

Ronnie was the newcomer, he joined the band in 1975 after Mick Taylor left. He played the clown, always joking around. He and his girlfriend Jo were great together. Jo was feisty and funny. She had told Ronnie when they first met that she worked in the broken-biscuit department at Woolworths. He actually went there looking for her, before he tracked her down. They were both naughty and mischievous and I loved them and had great fun hanging out with them. They always saw the funny side of things and they kept getting into trouble and recounting the tales. They were like naughty children.

Ronnie was very talented and a great guitar player – he'd already played with several very successful bands – but he was a serious alcoholic and doing a lot of drugs, so it was very hard to have an in-depth conversation with him. Everything was 'hey, hi, yeah'. It was hard to make a real connection. Keith and Ronnie were close – Keith had brought Ronnie into the band – and they got drunk and stoned together all night, every night.

Opposite: Bill and Charlie were both good friends who did a great job of keeping the band together. I really enjoyed spending time with them, whether backstage, on tour, or on holiday with the family.

I was always friendly with Bill. He was a bit of an outsider, like me, because neither of us took drugs. People who take drugs always want other people to join them and if you don't they treat you as if you're not cool. But the thing about being made to feel like an outsider is that it hurts your feelings. You're not quite part of the inner gang. So we bonded over that. Bill was quite a perfectionist with his music, he never missed a note; he was a brilliant bass player. He and Charlie were the solid rock for the rest of them, they were very professional, turning up at the studio on time and clear-headed and then waiting around for hours for the others to get there.

The Stones' marvellous drummer Charlie Watts is a lovely gentle guy who dressed like a Beau Brummel dandy. His waist was as small and elegant as his style icon Fred Astaire's and he had the shoes to match his outfits; handmade by Hobbs and beautifully polished. He travelled with a standing Louis Vuitton trunk, which he never unpacked, he just opened it and made sure the hangers were evenly spaced. He came to stay with us once, for a week. He followed me around the house talking to me while I folded clothes from the dryer. He kept putting everything straight – the pictures and the books and the nick-nacks.

Unlike the others, who found it hard to settle down, Charlie had married his wife Shirley in 1964, before the band got famous, and they are still together. He was always loyal to her and she was sweet and beautiful and elegant.

Charlie was often the wise, calm, cool-headed one who would turn up on time and sit for hours with his drumsticks, twirling them and keeping his fingers and wrists nimble, waiting for everyone else to get it together. I adored him – and I couldn't help noticing that Mick got a bit irritated by that.

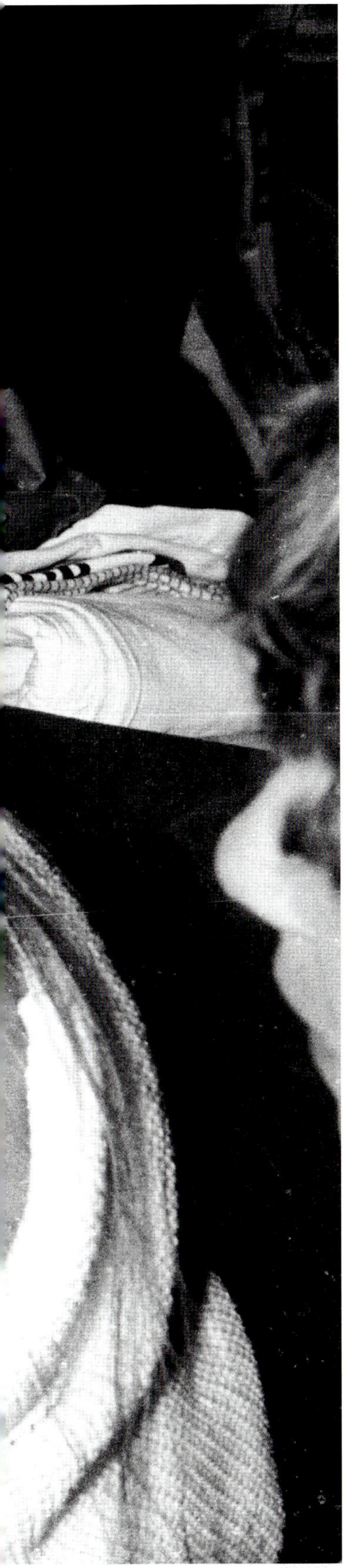

I was already pretty well-known in my own right, but the Stones' fame, and Mick's in particular, was on another level. They were the most famous, most successful band in the world and their every move was watched, written-about and recorded. We lived life in a goldfish bowl; the only way we ever got any privacy was behind closed doors, we had to have police escorts and every time we walked through a door or got out of a car, a dozen flashbulbs would go off in our faces.

Opposite: Mick and me shot by Norman Parkinson for People weekly, 1982.

7

LIFE WITH MICK

Our adventures, touring and travelling

had found my soul mate in Mick; we were so happy together. The Stones took a break from their recording in Paris and we spent Christmas in London at the Savoy and then went to Barbados and borrowed a friend's little wooden shack. I cooked and wore pink foam curlers in my hair and hung the clothes on the line while Mick played the guitar and tried out new songs on me.

We went back to Paris so that they could finish the *Some Girls* album and then we went to New York. We stayed in the Carlyle hotel; having fun, seeing friends and living together. I found Mick so easygoing; every day was playtime.

We saw a lot of Andy Warhol and Fred Hughes. Andy invited me to host his TV show which was on cable at three in the morning, so only a few drag queens saw it! We had no office and no meetings. Whenever we heard someone famous was in town, Andy and I would turn up, with a cameraman, and talk our way in. Andy told me not to ask about their work or anything important, so we talked about what they had for breakfast, or clothes, or gossip. We once interviewed Michael J Fox, who got cross and kicked us out when we didn't want to talk about his film.

Andy and I were also judges for the Cosmos Soccer Cheerleaders – we got to help choose girls to join the cheerleading squad for the Cosmos, who were a big New York team at the time. The Cosmos were owned by our friend Ahmet Ertegun, and he and his wife Mica took Mick and me under their wing. We started to be invited to big parties given by Pat Buckley and her husband Bill. As a child I had loved reading his newspaper column. He was the intellectual force behind the modern American Conservative movement, a dazzling writer who wrote about protecting a kind of American-Dream-Family-Life about which I could only fantasise.

We also saw a lot of Nan Kempner, who had the most beautiful couture clothes, and Lynn Wyatt, the Texan socialite, who was always especially kind to me. Through them we met Kenneth Jay Lane, who was camp and funny and designed gorgeous costume jewellery, dress designer Carolina Herrera and her husband, and Nancy and Ronald Reagan, who was then Governor of California and was already being talked about as a future president.

At the Kennedy Centre Honors, 1978.

Writer Gore Vidal wanted Mick to act in a film version of one of his books. Mica and Ahmet introduced us to Henry Kissinger and then took us to the fantastic new Kennedy Centre to see Marian Anderson and Fred Astaire get awards. We were sitting in a box next to that of the then-president

Jimmy Carter. I remember that I was wearing a beautiful biased-cut beige silk backless dress from Bill Blass. President Carter kept looking at me and smiling at me all night, and after the ceremony he made his way over to me, surrounded by secret service men, and said he wanted to be introduced. Ahmet introduced us and Mick said something but President Carter completely ignored him and said he had been admiring my beauty all night. He is definitely my favourite president!

Norman Parkinson, his wife Wanda and me at the Trinidad Carnival.

The Stones' new single *Miss You,* a song Mick had written about me, was a huge hit in America in May 1978 and created a huge demand for the Stones on tour. So a tour was booked and we all rented houses in Woodstock, New England, to rehearse.

Mick and I got there early and so did Keith. He had been to see a doctor in England who had given him something called the Black Box, which had electrodes that connected to Keith's ears. It was supposed to help break his heroin habit. He had been unable to quit and it was essential he did so because of the tour. So he went cold turkey on our couch and stayed there for a couple of weeks. He was very sick and slept a lot; it was like having a baby with us. I kept putting the electrodes back on his ears when they came off. As he got better, Mick and I looked on like proud parents. He got off heroin, but he was still taking coke and other drugs, so the positive effect was limited.

One day Mick was just about to go back to rehearsal when I pulled his arm and said, 'Don't go yet'. It was raining and I just had a bad feeling. He said, 'OK, I'll wait a minute'. As we stood watching the rain, a huge lightning bolt hit the big tree in our courtyard, just 10 feet away from us. The tree exploded and burst into thousands of sharp fiery fragments. The noise was deafening. Mick and I hung onto each other shaking. Later the rest of the band came over and looked at all the sharp spears sticking out of our house.

We set off on the tour and everywhere we went musicians and famous people would come backstage after the shows to hang out with us. Bob Dylan came in New York and in Chicago we met all the great Blues players. We went to see Muddy Waters playing in a club with Willie Dixon. The Stones were big fans; their Rhythm and Blues roots came from their mutual love of Muddy Waters' music. Muddy invited Keith and Mick and Woody on stage to play a few numbers with them. The boys loved it and we girls were so proud. It was a moment in musical history – a truly cool night!

There were a lot of spontaneous jamming sessions. One of the best was at Patti Boyd and Eric Clapton's wedding which took place at Eric's country house in 1979. The Stones got together with Eric, Rod Stewart, Paul McCartney, George Harrison and Ringo and they all played together all night. We danced until dawn. Mick and I were with his seven year-old daughter Jade, who was often with us, and we were due to stay the night, but hadn't been shown our room. We found an empty room with a four-poster bed and we all crashed out on it. In the morning, to our embarrassment, we found out we had collapsed in the bride and groom's room!

It was a lot of fun being on tour – travelling with the boys, sharing their after-show tales and jokes, sitting in the private plane after a successful show, feeling a common bond. It was like being part of a big family. But it was also hard work; all the travelling was physically and mentally exhausting. And the groupies were really irritating. Girls would sneak into the hotels and get backstage and throw themselves at the band. I had to watch out for them – they were ruthless and would do anything to get noticed! Often they would have sex with the security men just to get backstage passes.

By 1979 Mick and I had settled into New York living. We rented a lovely home and had great friends, but Mick wasn't touring and had too much time on his hands. He started going out a lot without me. He would say he had a meeting and then call to say it was running late. He had been linked with several girls in the gossip columns, but he denied it all, of course.

During this time I modelled for the big American designers such as Bill Blass and Oscar de La Renta. Oscar took me on trips to do fashion shows all over America and a couple of times to Japan. Being in the middle of all that success was like being in the eye of the storm. The phone rang constantly, as did the doorbell. I always had to answer it because Mick wouldn't – he was usually watching cricket on TV.

Mick and I moved out to Los Angeles for a while, and rented a house in a gated community near Bel Air. In LA we saw a lot of Eric Idle and the other Monty Python guys, the writer Ian La Frenais, and actor Robin Williams. We would have parties at each other's houses, and Robin Williams would get up and do hilarious improvisations. We would go over to Rod Stewart's house where he was living with Britt Ekland. They had red velvet furniture and leopard rugs and Tiffany lamps. We also hung out with George Hamilton and Alana, his Texan wife. George gave me the gold lamé and rhinestone outfit he'd worn in the film *Your Cheatin Heart* about the life of musician Hank Williams. Alana eventually divorced George and married Rod Stewart.

We all used to go to The Roxy Nightclub, where we got to know Jack Nicholson and Anjelica Huston. Anjelica and I became great friends, she was so smart, one of the funniest girls I had ever met. She too had her hands full, keeping an eye on Jack.

We often had Jade, Mick's daughter by Bianca, to stay. Bianca was a political activist and would leave Jade with us sometimes for weeks at a time, and once for a whole year. I loved having her, and we became very close. Mick had a second daughter I hadn't met yet. Karis was the daughter of actress Marsha Hunt, who had been a sensation in the musical *Hair* in London in the late sixties. When Karis came to stay with us, after Mick officially recognised her as his daughter, she was eleven and she was enchanting; a captivating mix of Mick and Marsha, who had done a great job of raising Karis on her own. Over the years I grew very fond of Karis and Marsha. Bianca also became a friend – I had a lot of respect for her and liked her a lot.

The Stones next album, *Emotional Rescue* was another huge hit. Around the time it came out I introduced Keith to a lovely model called Patti Hansen. They took one look at each other and that was that! I made Patti promise that she would keep Keith off heroin and she did.

After the album came out, Mick and I went to visit Norman Parkinson and his wife Wanda in Trinidad – we went over for the carnival and we all dressed up and joined in the procession; we were thrilled when our group won. We went on to have a holiday in Mustique and when we arrived back in New York there were two FBI agents waiting for us. They took us into a room at the airport and told us that John Lennon had been killed. Mick and I both started crying. John and Yoko lived next door to the apartment we rented in the Dakota building. We had hung out with him a few times and Mick loved him and his music. The FBI thought there might be a copycat killing and decided we needed protection. They had a man outside our apartment door for weeks, and we had to get a lawyer to get him to go. None of our friends wanted to come over, as they were nervous they might get busted.

Mick and I had been living like nomads for years, but we realised there was a pattern to our travel and we were starting to feel the need to settle down. We got on very well together, we never fought or argued and we shared a love of harmony and beauty. Our enthusiasm for buying houses seemed to be a natural part of that. The first house we bought in New York was a lovely old brownstone with original mouldings and fireplaces. We hired Jed Johnson, one of Andy Warhol's old boyfriends, to decorate. We also bought homes in Mustique, Amboise in France and London. It was time to settle down.

Below: In 1979 Mick and I went off to Brazil to do a musical film called Let's Spend the Night Together directed by Julien Temple and starring Dennis Hopper. In one scene I had to have a jealous fit and throw furniture out of the window of the Copacabana Hotel into the swimming pool. Art was very much imitating life!

Opposite: These were taken when Mick was recording at Chris Blackwell's place. He pulled my pants down and showed my bottom and then I pulled his down. We were just clowning around, and Johnny Pigozzi took the photos and sent them to us.

A Ranch of my Own

Despite living with a super-rich rockstar, I was always determined to earn my own living. I invested my first real money from modelling in racehorses and diamonds, definitely a girl's best friends!

During this time I did a commercial for Dr. Pepper soft drinks which was on TV nationwide everyday for six months. I was paid a lot of money and in 1981 I decided to use it to buy some land in Texas. I didn't often get a chance to go back to my home state, but I loved it and missed it and I wanted roots there.

Mick thought buying a ranch was a great idea. I was furious – and he laughed – when the press printed a story about him buying it for me as our fourth anniversary present. The only thing he bought me was the truck I used to drive around it.

My mother found the place for me: it was 500 acres and had a lake – water is always a prised possession in Texas – close to a small town called Lone Oak.

I loved that ranch. I had horses and cattle and played farmer, though it never made any money. We went as often as we could. Mick loved it because Lone Oak had a population of 300, they were all cattle and horse people and not one of them recognised him, so he could walk around like anyone else. And once we had kids we took them there so that they could run wild and free. I had that ranch for twenty-five years, then I sold it and bought a smaller place, just fifty acres, where my sister Rosy now lives.

Jerry Hall vient de prendre possession du ranch et des 300 acres (près de Dallas) que Mick lui a offerts pour le quatrième anniversaire de leur rencontre. En tête à tête, ça se voit.

JERRY HALL : POUR LEURS QUATRE ANNEES D'AMOUR, MICK JAGGER LUI OFFRE UN RANCH

ela ne vous dit vraiment
en ? Cherchez ! La
n rappelle l'Ange Bleu,
erry Hall, l'ange blond,
as la Marlène du Texas,
moins la
Ce n'est

séquence, c'est un instantané de la vie exemplaire de deux stars, une bouffée de spontanéité. Mick Jagger – toujours sobre – dont on n'aperçoit que le jean, vient d'offrir à Jerry Hall – ils

ranch de 300 acres dans la grande banlieue fourragère de Dallas où cette fille de camionneur possédait déjà 200 acres, acquises avec ses cachets de cover-girl qui lui ont

les délices d'une ville normale, mettait Mick en état de manque. Puisqu'il est amoureux, il a décidé de récidiver à « Lone Oak » qui n'est Jalna que pour Jerry. Jade, la fille qu'il a eue de Bianca Jagger, escortée de sa mammy, lui a fait promettre de revenir. Papa a promis. Jerry se réjouit : elle veut développer une nouvelle race de chevaux de course (elle monte depuis l'âge de cinq ans, bien avant Anne d'Angleterre), et sa sœur aînée monte en professionnelle de rodéo. Mick est tellement sensibilisé aux délices du corral qu'il va produire un film dans lequel il se réserve un petit rôle, la vedette étant, bien sûr, son grand amour. Le titre illustre à merveille leur contradiction : « Même les cow-girls peuvent avoir le cafard. » C'est aussi un titre de chanson.

Opposite: Mick's daughter Jade and me in old-fashioned Texan dress. The studio we were in specialised in historical photos and, as a card-carrying member of the Daughters of the Republic of Texas, I just couldn't resist a snap.

Above: Though I love this picture of me that appeared with an article for a French magazine, I didn't appreciate the reporting, which makes out that Mick bought my ranch for me! I was very proud of having bought it myself.
Left: Mick horsing around.

Exploring in Asia

Mick always had performer adrenaline withdrawals after his tours were over. He suffered a kind of depression which he liked to ward off with an adventure holiday. So as soon as the tour finished we would take off and discover some new corner of the world.

One of our favourite trips was to Kashmir in India. We went with Jade, and stopped in Singapore on the way. There we visited a cafe where all the 'girls' turned out to be transvestites! Mick was very happy, he loved being somewhere people didn't know him.

Kashmir is a wonderful region that straddles India and Pakistan, under the shadow of the world's greatest mountains, the Himalayas. In the foothills of the mountains it's cool and beautiful and we went pony trekking and camping. We spent Christmas on an enchanting houseboat on a lake surrounded by mountains. The lake was covered in lotus flowers and in the morning when the sun hit the beads of water on the flowers' green leaves, they sparkled like thousands of diamonds.

We also visited the Taj Mahal and I took a picture of Mick standing in front of it, wearing a hat, sunglasses and false moustache, as he often did when we were travelling – it was his way of avoiding any attention.

George Hurell

George Hurrell was almost 80 when we worked together. He had been a great Hollywood photographer who took pictures of almost every star over several decades. His striking black-and-white images were everywhere. He had retired in the seventies, but still worked when a project interested him. So I was flattered to be asked to pose for him for a series of photos in French *Vogue*.

George was extraordinary. He would style the picture, getting every fold perfect and then take one photograph with a big old-fashioned plate camera. Then he would say 'thank you' and help you down from the set. In one day he took 16 pages of photos – I had never seen that done before. While I was working with George and doing the Paris collections, Mick was shooting a film in the Amazon. When he wrote me the most wonderful love letter saying he was missing me, I knew I had to go and see him.

Dropping in on Mick up the Amazon

Mick was working on a film called *Fitzcarraldo*, deep in the Amazon jungle. We hadn't seen one another for weeks, and there was no phone where he was, so I hatched a plan to go and find him. I packed a bag and asked the editor of French *Vogue*, Francine Crescent, if she would give me a ticket to Lima, Peru and then on to Pulcallpa, where Mick had said he was. I told her that if she gave me some swimsuits, a camera and some film, I would get Mick to do some photos of me on the Amazon. She said yes, and off I flew. When I arrived in Pulcallpa the only hotel was full, but they let me sleep on a cot in a maid's room. The next morning I talked a pilot into taking me in his small plane to look for Mick. I had very little money on me, so I promised him that Mick would pay him when we got there. Amazingly, he agreed!

We took off, following the vast Amazon River, thousands of miles of jungle stretching out before us, hoping to see the boat that Mick was on. The pilot was just about to turn back we rounded a bend and saw the boat. We found a field and managed a bumpy landing, and then some Indians – stark naked apart from their bright red paint – gave us a ride in their canoe. We came silently up to Mick's camp, where he was sitting playing backgammon with a blonde girl. I pointed my finger at Mick and said, 'aha, caught you!' Mick ran up, lifting me out of the canoe, hugging and kissing me. He said he had never been so happy to see anyone. The blonde turned out to be another actor's wife. They were all amazed to see me, having had no contact with the outside world for weeks.

I stayed for the next couple of months. We slept under a mouldy piece of blue plastic and it rained every day – our clothes were constantly wet. Mick did manage to take some great photographs of me, lounging in leopard-print swimsuits on tree branches that overhung the Amazon. Even Bailey was impressed with the photos when they appeared in French *Vogue*.

Sadly Jason Robards, the leading actor, caught severe dysentery and couldn't complete the film – so the director Werner Herzog brought in Klaus Kinski and re-shot the whole thing. Mick was already under contract to do a Stones tour, so he couldn't do the re-shoot. All that time and hard work and nothing to show for it.

Above & Left: The dappled sunlight that came through the rainforest canopy gave a beautiful effect to these shots, which ended up in French Vogue. David Bailey was so impressed by the photos that Mick took of me in this leopard-print swimsuit that he even asked him what F-stop he had used. Opposite: A snap of the Molly Aida, the steamer central to the plot of Fitzcarraldo.

Andy Warhol: A Close Friendship

I met Andy in Paris when I was 16 and I knew him until he died 15 years later. He was a dear friend, I loved him. He had founded *Interview* magazine, which was very popular with the in-crowd. He asked me to be on the cover, and I was happy to say yes, it was a cool, interesting magazine.

Andy was a little bit nerdy, he didn't take drugs, he wasn't cool looking, and he was gay and religious, but somehow he made himself cool anyway. He was a lovely guy, with a very kind heart. He came to all our family get-togethers and always brought presents for the children.

We liked a lot of the same things. I used to go to the flea market to collect brightly coloured fifties pop art Fiestaware plates and he did too. He was very visual and not that articulate, he didn't speak a lot. He liked to gossip, but he didn't like to have intellectual conversations. He wouldn't explain why he liked something. He'd say 'golly' and 'gee whizz' all the time. He loved odd things – like that Japanese fake plastic food some restaurants have in the window. And he was impressed with cities, factories and assembly lines – he loved the film *Metropolis*. Andy was very religious, super-spiritual, that was one of the things I liked about him. He was Catholic and he would often go to church and light candles. He made his portraits like icons, with a spiritual quality to them. I loved the *Last Supper*, one of his final paintings.

Andy liked to talk about odd things, which I enjoyed. He always said he felt sorry for the space that he was inhabiting. We could talk that kind of nonsense, and it made you think. He had a different kind of mind. He was quirky.

Andy collected things. Everywhere he went he took a matchbox or a napkin and at the end of the day he put everything in a ziplock sandwich bag and labelled it. Then he put them all in boxes and put them in storage. His house was beautiful, all dark wood and very chic, but he had rooms and rooms full of the junk he collected, he was an obsessive collector. And he tape-recorded everything. I was lucky, I came off quite well in his book, but some people came off very badly indeed.

Interview
July
$1.00

Andy loved glamour and famous people and movie stars. He loved to be around them, but he was shy too, so he would often stand quietly in the corner, just watching. He loved to go out because he didn't want to miss anything, he loved gossip and hearing what everyone was up to.

When Mick was away touring, Andy or Fred, his business manager and partner, would be my escort. We went out a lot. We'd often go to Studio 54, the happening place in New York then, and meet up with actors, artists, models and musicians. Mick would leave me upstairs with Andy and Fred and go off on his own.

Andy hung out a lot with Truman Capote and Tennessee Williams, who hated each other. Andy hated that and wished they could be friends. People who write about him and make documentaries sometimes make him out to be wicked, but he wasn't at all. He didn't hurt people.

Left: New Year's day, 1978, a party at Studio 54 and Blondie. I think some of them had been there since New Year's Eve! With Bob Colacello (publisher of Interview Magazine), Andy Warhol, Debbie Harry, Truman Capote and Paloma Picasso.

Above: Andy and me celebrating New Year, 1978, at Studio 54. I feel so blessed that we were such good friends for over 20 years. Andy's talent and uniqueness were so inspiring. Someone like Andy can never be replaced.

Andy wanted people to get his art instantly. He resented the idea of people having to have an art degree and discuss art, he felt it should be for the masses and they should be able to look at your art and get it without being educated or knowing anything about art. I liked that, he was very democratic. He didn't like people trying to intellectualise his art. He liked to confuse the media and not tell them anything about it.

I don't think he planned what he was doing. Take the Campbell's soup can. A lot of 'experts' said it was some kind of statement about consumerism, but I think it was much simpler than that. Andy actually ate Campbell's tomato soup every day. In his kitchen he had a cupboard full of cans of soup. He painted it because he looked at it every single day and it was his favourite food. He trusted it.

Andy asked me to sit for him and did two portraits – each of them in three different colours. He took the photos and then created the paintings with a silk screen. I loved the portraits. The blue one is really pretty. Andy did my mouth as it actually is, whereas with some people he did a slight shift and made them look a bit scary.

He had all these young guys that he would pick up. He would dress them in big boots and jeans with suspender belts and no shirt, or a T-shirt, and then give them giant paint guns – it was all very sexual. The guns were to spray-paint different bits of whatever he was working on, he'd tell them which colours to do. Even more bizarre were his 'piss' paintings. He'd get a cute guy to come in off the street and piss on the painting. It was something to do with the urine oxidising the paint. He said I should take one of the finished works, but I didn't want it! He got a big kick out of getting these cute guys in. He was always trying something new. Andy died when Lizzie was three and Jimi just one – Andy adored them, he was a great family friend and we missed him.

Above: Me by Andy Warhol, red lipstick firmly in place!

The Dark Side of Fame

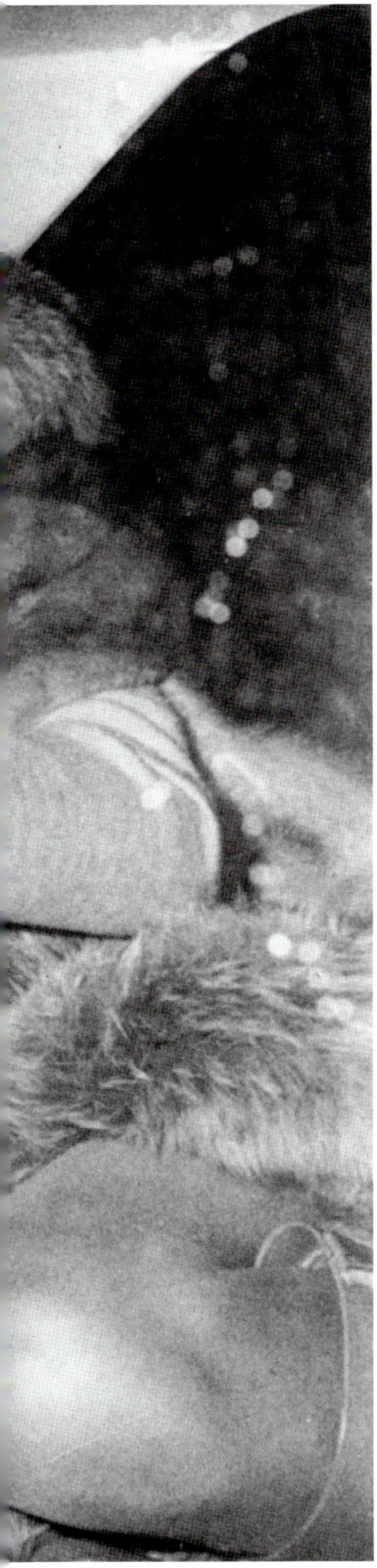

There was a downside to fame. We didn't mind being looked at and photographed, but The Stones seemed to attract a lot of kooky people, and that could be quite frightening.

One St. Patrick's Day, Mick and I decided to go for a walk in the park and have a late lunch at the Plaza Hotel. As we were walking along holding hands in the sunshine, people started to recognise Mick. There had been a St. Patrick's Day parade and a lot of drinking going on. Louts started to shout at us, so we picked up our pace and were almost at the Plaza when the crowd began chasing us. We ran, but the mob caught up with us. They pulled off my beret and with it some hair that it was pinned to; they took our scarves and ripped our coats. Mick tried to fight them off, but they engulfed us and we were screaming for help. Eventually some policemen came to our rescue. They pulled Mick free of the crowd and he was yelling, 'She's with me'. Then they pulled me out and, using their shields and batons, they got us, bleeding and shaking, into the Plaza. After that I was scared to go out for a while.

Another time, when we were touring in Ireland, the band had a death threat from the IRA. Mick and I went for a walk to talk about it and Mick had an anxiety attack. He couldn't breathe, so we called a doctor who made Mick breathe into a paper bag. What with the death threats and the crazy fans, not to mention some attacks in the press, it was difficult not to feel isolated, and even a bit paranoid, during this period.

VAT
Watkin
APOLOGISE FOR
INCONVENIENCE
CAUSED DUE TO
THESE WOR
BEING
CARRIED OUT

Left: Up among the rooftops of Paris, photographed by Patrick Demarchelier for French Vogue.

8

FASHION, STAGE & SCREEN

Filming with Jack Nicholson, treading the boards in New York and Fashion Aid

I've always loved earning my own living, no matter whether there was a man in my life or not. So when I was with Bryan, and then settling down with Mick, I carried on working and paying my own way.

I modelled right though the eighties, both on the catwalks and for magazines. By the nineties I was more interested in acting and I only did Vivienne Westwood and Thierry Mugler's shows on the catwalk.

I've always had a parallel interest in acting, and that's the direction I began to pursue seriously in the eighties. My very first acting part was when I was in Paris aged 16. I had a small part in a Roger Vadim film called *St. Germaine de Pres après la Guerre*, in which I was in the Café de Flore, talking to several old gentlemen about World War Two.

When I was 18 and living in New York I started taking acting lessons at The Actors' Studio with Stella Adler. Shelly Winters was giving some classes, and we made friends. She was a wonderful actress and a great teacher and I was so lucky to get to know her. I think she'd had some bad luck with men, because she gave me lots of advice and warnings!

I got a small walk-on part in *Marathon Man*, directed by John Schlesinger and starring Dustin Hoffman and Laurence Olivier, but in the end my part was cut out of the movie, although I didn't find that out until I was at the premiere in London with Bryan Ferry.

When I moved to London I studied acting at the National Theatre with Kate Fleming and voice with Patsy Rodenburg. And when I was living in New York with Mick I started to get the odd acting job.

I was invited on the David Letterman show a couple of times and I told him that my Mama taught me that 'the way to keep a man was to be a maid in the living room, a cook in the kitchen and a whore in the bedroom'. I told him that I would hire the first two and do the last bit myself! This quote got into the *Oxford Dictionary of Humorous Quotations*, which was pretty cool!

When Mick and I went to Los Angeles, everyone we met was in the movie business and we both kept getting approached about film projects. I went back to acting school and I got parts in a couple of my Texan friend Shelly Duvall's 'Fairy Tale Theatre' films – *Jack and The Beanstalk*, in which I played a golden harp, and *The Emperor and The Nightingale*. In that one Mick played the Chinese Emperor and Anjelica Huston and I played fairies with pointy ears. Mick and I also did a promotional film, directed by Hal Ashby, called *Running out of Luck*.

In 1980 I got a part in the film *Urban Cowboy*, starring John Travolta. I played one of his girlfriends and my sister Cyndy was in it too. We had a lot of fun and it was a big hit. After that I started to get more parts and I had several small film roles. All my acting jobs, like my modelling work, had to be fitted around having babies, because in the mid-eighties

I had two children, Lizzy and Jimi, in eighteen months. It was a few months after Jimi's birth that I went to Italy to make *Galileo Mouse*, playing a nuclear physicist.

In Los Angeles I did a film with Eddie Murphy called *Vampire in Brooklyn* and in the South of France I worked on a film called *RPM*. Roman Polanski's wife Emmanuelle Seigner was in it and he came to visit her. We all went to dinner one night with Helmut and June Newton in Monte Carlo.

With Annie Lennox at Fashion Aid, 1985.

My most recent film was for the BBC; the dramatisation of a Martin Amis book called *Money*, directed by Jeremy Lovering and starring Nick Frost. I played a Mrs. Robinson-type actress; it was dark and funny and I had a great time doing it.

I took time out from acting to have two more babies, and then went back to what I love most – the theatre. I prefer the stage to film because you're more in control, you know what's happening. With film it jumps around, you film the end before the beginning, so you don't know what's going to come out at the end. I love Hitchcock movies where it's one long scene and you're drawn in, rather than endless scene changing.

Throughout the eighties and nineties I did a series of plays – *Bus Stop* in New York and London, *Benchmark*, *High Society*, *Love Letters* with David Soul in Ireland and the one that really made my name in theatre, *The Graduate*. I played Mrs. Robinson in London, New York and more recently, Australia. I went on to be in plays such as *The Vagina Monologues*, *Picasso's Women* and *The Play What I Wrote*. All challenging, all demanding and all enormously fulfilling.

I was always working. In the mid-eighties I made a commercial for L'Oreal with Bailey, and we also did two for Bovril – chicken Bovril and beef Bovril. I had the craziest outfits. I also wrote my first autobiography *Tall Tales* and made a yoga exercise video.

It was in the late eighties that Madame Tussauds approached me about making my waxwork model. It's extraordinary how they measure every tiny part of you and then match your hair and eyes. It's a bit scary to look at yourself like that. There was a press launch, with me standing next to it, and even my children found it disconcerting. It's on permanent exhibition, which is nice, though I'm glad to say they sometimes change its clothes!

David Bailey: A Lifelong Friend

David Bailey is the most wonderful photographer to work with. We have had so many good times, producing such glorious photographs together. His sharp, pared down, tightly cropped and gritty monochrome images transform his sitters into heroic figures. He gave me a shot he had taken of Bob Dylan which is one of my favourite photographs of all time. And I have always loved the photos he has taken of me.

One of the things I love most about Bailey is his integrity. If he doesn't feel inspired by a job, he turns it down – no matter how much money is on offer. Bailey has dyslexia and, while not always adept at articulating his thoughts verbally, he is a visual genius. He left school at 15 and learned his art by becoming a photographer's assistant, and by his early twenties he was taking pictures for *Vogue*. Because he works so instinctively, clients have to trust him and let him do his job – and he always produces stunning photographs. He is also a film-maker, and has won awards for his television commercials and short anti-fur films. He is passionately against the killing of animals for their fur.

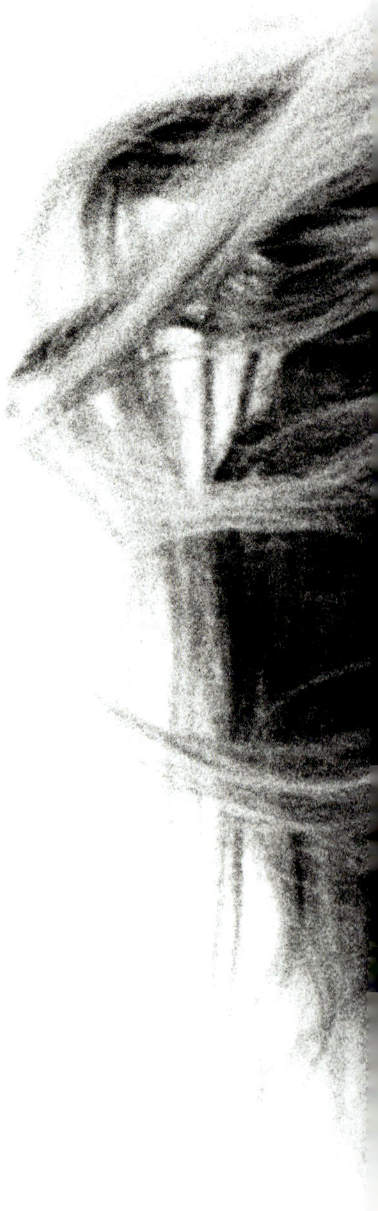

Right: Bailey took this photo of me putting the final touches to my makeup before a shoot and it's one of my favourites. I love the way that he has managed to capture that last moment of focused calm that exists before a job begins.

One of the most memorable shoots Bailey and I did together was for French *Vogue*, in the south of France. We went with the great artist and photographer Jacques Henri Lartigue, who was then in his late eighties. Lartigue had been famous in his youth for his images of the privileged world of France at the turn of the century. His photographs of horse drawn carriages, early automobiles and glamorous women and their friends had really captured an era.

He had been re-discovered in his seventies in New York and had started working for *Vogue*. When I met him he was an adorable smiling, white haired gentleman who took snaps of me while Bailey photographed us both. Later I called his wife begging for one of those photos, but she told me that sadly they hadn't come out well. I'd have loved to have seen them.

Opposite: With Lartigue for French Vogue.

Terence Donovan

I did a lot of work with Terence after I came to live in London. He was one of the original celebrity photographers in London along with David Bailey and Brian Duffy. Between them they captured and helped to create the swinging sixties that made London the fashion and style centre of the world. Terence was a lovely guy, and great fun to work with. He'd take the photos quite quickly, get it all sewn up and then we'd go out and have caviar for lunch and he'd entertain us with stories. He was a black belt in judo and wrote a book about it, and he used to tell me about it. He was an adventurous photographer, who always loved to try something new. I was terribly sad when I heard he'd died at the age of 60 – far too young.

Right & Following pages: Harpers & Queen, 1978. Terence was great at capturing that Hollywood era that I love so much but with a slick, contemporary twist.

Patrick Lichfield

Patrick and his lovely wife Leonora were neighbours of ours on Mustique. They were often there at the same time as us, and their children were similar ages to ours, so I knew him first as a friend. We'd all get together at people's houses for dinner and games, and Patrick and Leonora were great fun. He was an extremely well-known photographer, though we only did the occasional job together. One of them was an advertisement for the Mandarin Oriental Hotel chain, which we shot in Laguna Beach, California, with me in a cowboy hat and a white shirt standing in the desert. On the day we had to shoot it one of my children was sick and I had to stay in the hotel, so Patrick shot the background and then came and shot me and superimposed the two. It was very successful and is still running all these years later.

Above: Patrick always recorded a crew photo after every shoot. This one belongs to the Mandarin Oriental shoot with me in the cowboy hat (see page 2) that I had to be superimposed onto at the last minute. Opposite: In high heels, diamonds and furs – what more could a girl want?

Left: Outside the Groucho Club at a photocall to promote Fashion Aid with Bruce Oldfield, Jasper Conran and Scott Crolla, amongst others. **Opposite:** Getting ready backstage at the Royal Albert Hall with Marie Helvin, Anjelica Huston, Grace Jones, David Bailey and Mick. **Following pages:** Applying the final touches to Anjelica's make-up.

Fashion Aid

In November 1985 I was invited to take part in Fashion Aid – a huge fashion extravaganza in London's Albert Hall – in aid of famine relief. It was our good friend Bob Geldof who asked us and of course I wanted to be part of it. Mick had already appeared in Bob's Live Aid concert, four months earlier, and this was part of the same effort to help people who were starving in Africa. Fashion Aid was to feature the world's top designers and models. There were 18 designers taking part, but I knew there was only one man who could design me an outfit that would stand out in a venue as huge as the Albert Hall, and that was my friend Anthony Price, a master of showmanship. I had first met him when he designed the mermaid outfit for me to wear on the *Siren* album cover and we'd been friends ever since. Now I needed something spectacular that people could appreciate while looking down from the tiered seating above us. I talked to Anthony and he got straight to work.

Anthony came up with a creation that was simply wonderful – a tightly-fitting dress with a huge tiered skirt. And to show it off, he arranged for me to be carried onto the stage in a curtained sedan, held aloft by two gorgeous young men in pink satin!

We all had enormous fun backstage. My dear friends Marie Helvin and Anjelica Huston took part, and it was wonderful to see old friends like Grace Jones. Mick was there behind the scenes, helping out and making us all laugh. There was a lot of champagne drinking going on. There were so many of us! As well as the designers and models, there were 60 make-up artists, 35 hairdressers, and over 100 assistants. Each of the designers was given 15 minutes to show their designs so the whole thing went on for several hours.

The show was a huge success, the Albert Hall was packed and it raised a huge sum for famine relief.

My spectacular entrance went down very well and everyone else was very jealous! Anthony was in heaven because it brought the house down. He came on at the end and loved it.

Opposite: Making my grand entrance, complete with very special pink satin-clad helpers. **Right:** Lapping up the applause with a delighted Anthony Price at the finale.

Above: The premier of Urban Cowboy. This outfit, gold lamé with rhinestones, was the one George Hamilton gave me; he had worn it in the film about the life of Hank Williams. I loved it. Right: With Cyndy, director Jeff Bridges and a (very hairy) John Travolta on the Urban Cowboy set. Opposite page: Two Saturday Night Live skits; one singing Stand by Your Man with Dame Edna and wearing my gold lamé outfit, the other wearing the outfit Anthony Price made me for a chicken Bovril advert I did with Bailey. It had a huge feather tail, like a bird of paradise.

Large and Small Screen Performances

In New York I was lucky enough to be asked by Lorne Michaels to host NBC's *Saturday Night Live* and I had so much fun doing the live comedy. Mick was in one skit with me – we neither of us minded laughing at ourselves. I also appeared with Edna Everage, singing a duet, and in the chicken outfit I'd worn for the Bovril commercial I did with David Bailey.

After that I was called to audition for a film to be shot in Texas called, *Urban Cowboy*. In Texas, 'urban cowboy' was considered a derogatory term for cowboys who weren't proper cowboys – they were all hat and no cattle! Jeff Bridges – the director, not the actor – made the film and John Travolta was starring. I played one of John's girlfriends, with a big scene in Gilly's Nightclub and then a *ménage a trois* in bed with John. I talked them into hiring my sister Cyndy who was living in New York at that time. We went down to Houston to film and we had a great time with John, who was sweet but hairy! The film was a big hit and Andy Warhol came as my date to the premiere and after-party at Gilly's.

Above left: On-screen with a very menacing Jack Nicholson. **Above right:** All made-up and ready for my scene with Kim Basinger. **Opposite:** Batman was such a huge blockbuster that I found myself appearing in all kinds of spin-off merchandise including this DC comic of which my youngest, Gabriel, is very proud.

Batman

I was filming a chocolate candy bar commercial at Shepperton film studio when I chatted with a charming man who said he was doing the set design on a new movie called *Batman* and that I must meet the director Tim Burton. Sure enough I had a meeting with Tim Burton; he was wonderful, full of mad, contagious, creative juices. I got the part of Alicia Hunt, a gangster's moll who is horribly disfigured by the Joker, played by Jack Nicholson.

I turned up for work and had coffee with Michael Keaton who was playing Batman. I wore clothes designed by Anthony Price and Azzedine Alaia. The film was dark and interesting, and I loved working with Tim Burton. He's an actor's director; he gets everything ready and lets you go with it. I was already friends with Jack Nicholson. Tim Burton and I would be on set getting the lights perfect and Jack would come on and change it all to his advantage. I guess that's how Hollywood stars stay on top. He would have my back to the camera looking over his shoulder while he was looking in the mirror when I was saying my lines. But the film was a huge hit and led to a lot of other film parts.

HE...
HE'S GONE.
--DISTRICT ATTORNEY HARVEY DENT PROMISES TO WAGE WAR ON BOSS CARL GRISSOM--
PRETTY TOUGH TALK ABOUT CARL.
DON'T WORRY ABOUT IT, ALICIA. IF THIS CLOWN DENT COULD TOUCH GRISSOM--
--I'D HAVE KILLED HIM BY NOW.
IF GRISSOM KNEW ABOUT US... HE MIGHT KILL YOU.
DON'T FLATTER YOURSELF, ANGEL. HE CAN'T RUN THIS CITY WITHOUT ME.
AND BESIDES, HE DOESN'T KNOW.
YOU LOOK FINE.
I DIDN'T ASK.

Bus Stop

I was so happy when I was offered the part of Cherie, a pretty young singer, in the play *Bus Stop* in New York. I was playing opposite Markus Flanagan, who played Bo, the young cowboy Cherie falls for when their bus is snowed in and they have to spend the night in a café with six other people. Mick came to the opening with his parents. I was very nervous appearing on stage, but I loved it – there's nothing as exciting as live theatre because it's so thrilling to have an audience. I love comedy most of all; when the audience laughs it is instant gratification.

Marilyn Monroe had played the part of Cherie in the film version and it wasn't easy following her! But I got a very good review from Frank Rich of the *New York Times*, and as a result British producer Michael White asked me to transfer with the play when it moved to London's West End. Markus Flanagan was so good, but Michael hired Shaun Cassidy instead, as he was better known in England. We opened in Watford in 1989 and then moved on to the Lyric Theatre in the West End. The reviews were mixed but we ran for four months to full houses.

Top left: In the dressing room with Shaun Cassidy. **Middle left:** Going over my lines with Markus Flanagan. **Top right & Middle right:** On stage in my fabulous showgirl costume. **Bottom:** At an afterparty for Bus Stop with Mick's parents, Joe and Eva.

Annie Liebovitz

Annie was the chief photographer for *Rolling Stone* magazine for ten years, so she photographed Mick and the rest of the Stones a lot. Mick knew her well and it was through him that I got to know her. Then she was asked to do some work for *Vanity Fair* and we began working together.

I always enjoyed working with Annie, she had lots of energy and enthusiasm and she took fabulous pictures. We both loved old-style, sexy pin-up photos and when I suggested we do a pin-up calendar together Annie loved the idea. We designed the whole thing between us; I got the clothes and created the outfits and Annie put together the backgrounds and images. It was great to work closely with her and I loved the end results – the pictures were fun and sexy. We had to hurry to get all 12 months shot, because I was pregnant at the time, with Jimi, and my stomach was getting bigger every day.

This page: A few polaroids from the calendar. **Opposite:** May, my favourite shot in the calendar – a Jane Russell moment – and a great pair of cowboy boots.

Left: With the designer and dressed to kill in a sequined evening gown and sheer wrap at Thierry Mugler's swatch-covered studio in Paris. **Opposite:** I love the way that Thierry's clothes ooze sex appeal, like this beautifully cut black ball gown that I modelled for his 1995 catalogue.

Thierry Mugler

Thierry Mugler is one of my favourite designers, we worked together closely for over 20 years. I adore him; he doesn't do couture any more, but for years he made such sexy clothes, he is a genius and was so ahead of his time. Thierry is a real artist and his clothes were more works of art than practical clothes you can wear. He was always mesmerised by old Hollywood glamour and drew a line from that lost era to the era of sexual liberation. His clothes often had broad shoulders and wasp waists, they were so feminine.

Thierry adored iconic women and they turned up in his extravagant fashion shows. He loved the artifice of the blonde; the cosmetically produced woman who has something about her that implies a secret and even a malign seductiveness. His shows were more performance art than fashion show. I loved working with him. Thierry is also a talented photographer, I always enjoyed a shoot with him, and his fashion shows were the first thing I did when I went back to work after Georgia May's birth.

I was thrilled when Thierry asked me to be the model for his Angel Perfume. We did the photos in Death Valley Desert in the States – near the place where they tested the first nuclear bombs. Shooting the photos – which Thierry took himself – was extraordinary. I had to lie across the sand, looking seductive and perfectly groomed, without disturbing a grain of sand, so that he could capture the ripples of the desert. I lay there for literally hours, trying to look fresh and poised while wilting in the heat! Thierry wanted to capture the photo at sunset, so he had a tungsten spotlight on me. It wasn't the easiest shoot I've ever done, but it was worth it because the results were stunning – the sand looked perfect! And the perfume has been a huge success. I love it, it smells of chocolate and vanilla and sex.

Left: Melting in the Nevada Desert, in furs, at sunset. Along with the Siren cover shoot for Roxy Music, this was one of the most difficult shoots I have done. **Opposite:** The final result, which made all the waiting around in the heat worthwhile. I love the way the wavy curls in my hair are set off by the ripples in the sand. **Below:** Lizzie, Jimi and one very over-excited parent with the finished poster.

Opposite: Our young family. Holidaying in Barbados with Mick and our two eldest children Lizzie and James, photographed by Norman Parkinson.

9

FAMILY LIFE

Our Balinese wedding and bringing up four beautiful children

Mick and I had our first baby, Elizabeth, in March 1984 and we both adored her. We took her to Mustique when she was three weeks old. I was so carefree and was mesmerised by my baby. I loved breastfeeding and letting her hear the noise of the waves, lying on a blanket looking at the trees and sky and flowers. Mick left to go back to work and Elizabeth and I stayed for four months. It was a joyous time for me.

I took Elizabeth to Texas to meet my mother and sisters, and then Mick and I took her to London to meet his parents and to have her christened. I loved Mick's parents, Eva and Joe; they were very kind and supportive. Eva had a great sense of family and telephoned often, getting us all together regularly. She loved music and enjoyed a good knees up. As she'd had two boys, she treated her other son Chris's wife Kari-Ann and me like daughters. She loved to have a natter, and she was helpful with domestic issues such as cooking, household management and child rearing, although she never wanted to talk about personal problems regarding her sons. Joe was a history and physical education teacher and he liked to give a little history lesson while going for a long walk. I felt very affectionate towards them; they were good down-to-earth people who welcomed me with open arms.

When Elizabeth was nine months old we went to Brazil to make a rock promotion film. We took a break on an island off the coast and while there I got pregnant again. When we got back to New York I went for a scan and the doctor told me I was pregnant with twins. Mick nearly fainted when I told him. I was overjoyed, but also had to come to grips with the idea of feeding and looking after two babies plus Elizabeth.

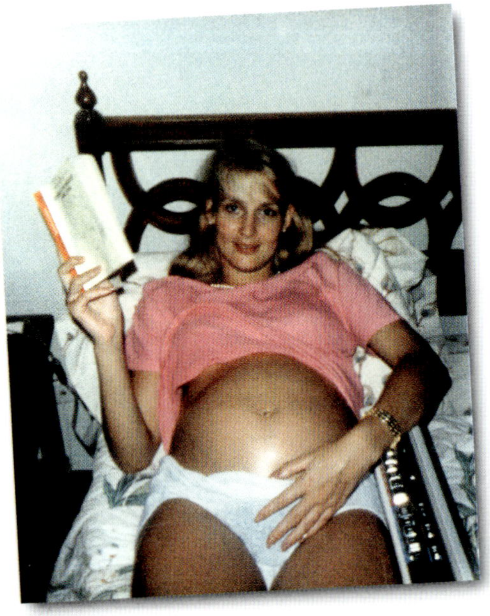

I was still modelling; I made a calendar with Annie Leibovitz and a commercial for Budweiser Beer. But at three months pregnant I went for another scan to discover that one twin was slightly bigger than the other. At five months I had a bit of bleeding and another scan. One baby's heart had stopped beating. I kept bleeding and had to stay in bed lying down as I had a blood clot where the remaining baby's placenta connected to my uterus. It was very difficult to stay in bed and not be able to look after Elizabeth and the emotional stress of losing one of my babies was painful. While I was stuck in bed, Mick was asked by Bob Geldof to do the Live Aid concert to raise money for Africa. It was televised worldwide and it was the most amazing concert. I was so proud of Mick, who sang a song with Tina Turner.

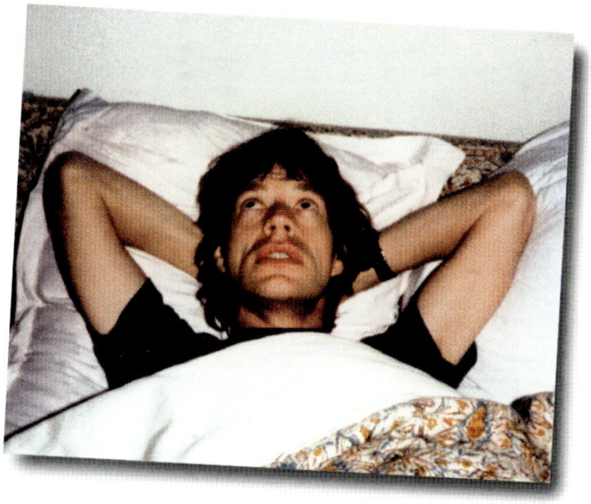

Mick and I rented a house in upstate New York to spend the summer out of the heat and to wait for our baby to be born. Karis was spending the summer with us, and one night when Mick was at work in the studio and Karis and I were watching TV and eating pizza, I went into labour with James. Karis and I rushed into New York to Lennox Hill Hospital and Mick met us there. I had a natural birth as I had done with Elizabeth, and James was born August 28th, 1985, a healthy and gorgeous baby. Tina Turner sent him a black bear with a nametag saying 'Jimi Jagger'. But I suffered postnatal depression probably caused by mourning for my dead child and not being able to talk about it as we had kept it all a secret.

James was such a good baby and Elizabeth was so sweet with her new little brother. I was occupied with them both while Mick was busy, often leaving me at home on my own with the babies.

We went to London and had James christened in the same Church where Elizabeth had been christened. Jack Nicholson and Anjelica Huston were his godparents and David Bailey took the christening photos.

Mick and I took Elizabeth and James to our house in France. We were having fun with the babies and Mick was writing songs and working in a studio he had set up in the chapel. The French photographer Guy Boudin came and took some splendid photos and a cover of me for *Best* magazine. He was so talented and got very excited roaming around finding locations and getting ideas for photos. We did shoots with Elizabeth and James and they looked so adorable.
I kept hearing stories of Mick's dalliances with other women. Mick was a dangerous sexual predator and, although I loved him and he swore undying love for me, I felt very unsure of him. I had weaned him off drugs, but they had been replaced by sex and he had never had proper treatment. Even in our early days together, my instincts told me that he could not help indulging himself with other women and by the time we had children I would read about Mick's dalliances in the newspapers.

I decided I would settle in England, on my own if need be. I rented a house in London and when I was offered a part playing a nuclear physicist in a film called *Galileo Mouse*, I took it. It was in Italy and I had learned Italian, but in the end they over-dubbed me with the same woman who did the voice of Sophia Loren.

After filming I took the children to stay with friends in Tuscany for a few weeks holiday. Mick had been calling me a lot, telling me how he had changed, and that he loved me and missed me and wanted to marry me in Bali. I still loved him very much, so I said yes, and

A page from Punch magazine.

we set about planning a wonderful trip that would take in Nepal, Bhutan, Thailand and Bali.

I had heard rumours that Mick had stolen Eric Clapton's girlfriend, Carla Bruni, and had started an affair with her. Mick denied it, saying it was nothing and that he loved me and was marrying me. So I stifled my doubts and went ahead with our trip. We flew from London to Frankfurt, then on to Kathmandu, in Nepal, with Elizabeth who was six and James who was five. We also took a nanny, a tutor and Alan Dunn, a bodyguard, who was in charge of our twenty-six suitcases, and logistics.

In Kathmandu we slept in tree houses, rode elephants and saw tigers. We then went on the Prince Charles Trek, so named because the Prince took the trek before his marriage to Diana. It was 40 kilometres in three days, mostly uphill. Elizabeth walked stoically the whole way without ever complaining. Jimi, who was only five years old, had to be carried some of the way. By the time we got back to our hotel we were exhausted.

After 10 days in Nepal we flew to the tiny kingdom of Bhutan. Mick had met the Queens of Bhutan (three beautiful sisters who were all married to the King) on a flight and they had invited him to visit. It was freezing cold and the air was very thin, but it was so glorious, on the top of the world surrounded by snow-peaked mountains. We had yak tea in the Palace with the beguiling Queens. From Bhutan we went to Bangkok, Thailand and then on to Bali, where we were to marry.

We had some friends in Bali – the decorator Linda Garland, her ex-husband Amir and his new wife Hippolyta and they helped Mick to organise it. Everything was to be a surprise for me; I was longing to know, but Mick wouldn't tell me anything. Bali is largely Hindu, so first of all we had a ceremony in which we converted to Hinduism; of course, I didn't understand anything, but just did as I was told!

Our wedding was beautiful; a traditional Balinese Hindu ceremony. But sadly the day after we married, to my dismay Mick took off for Japan, where he said he had an award to collect. I took the children and the luggage back to London and then on to our house in New York, where I threw myself into work. I did my first play, *Bus Stop* and when the play ended I took Lizzie and Jimi to Mustique and then off to Atlanta, Georgia, where Mick was recording an album. It was in Georgia that I became pregnant with our third child. We went back to England and rented a house in Barnes and then Mick bought us a beautiful eighteenth century house on Richmond Hill where we spent our time decorating and waiting for the birth.

Georgia was born in January 1992 – another healthy, beautiful baby and I was so happy.

I took Georgia home and when she was two weeks old we flew to Mustique with Lizzie and Jimi, a tutor and a nanny to spend a few months there. That same year my close friend Anjelica Huston married sculptor Robert Graham Junior. Anjelica asked all the guests to wear cream.

Mick and I loved our new house in Richmond, but although Mick wanted his children educated in England, he was a tax exile and so could only be with us for a short time each year. When he was home we had so much fun. We took the children and dog for long walks in the park to look at the deer and at night we would get into bed and I would put my foot next to Mick's big warm foot and feel so much love and happiness and peace. And in the morning I would wake up to Mick bringing me a cup of tea.

But it was only ever for a while, because of Mick's tax situation. The Stones continued to tour and the tours got longer and longer and I could no longer just uproot the children and take them along. And when he was with us he took a long time to get back into family life. Over a ten-year period the Rolling Stones went on five major world tours. Mick kept himself so busy that he started to miss important family events – school holidays, children's birthdays and our anniversary. I was especially heartbroken that he wasn't home in time for the birth of our fourth child, Gabriel.

We had met up for the children's Easter break at a dude ranch in west Texas and I got pregnant with Gabriel while we were visiting Presidio, the hottest town in America, close to the Mexican border. After we got home Mick went off to tour again and I spent most of my pregnancy in Richmond with the children.

Gabriel was born naturally on December 9th, 1997 after a very long labour. One of my neighbours had taken me to the hospital. Mick called while I was in labour to say he was so sorry not to be there. He arrived home a week later. He was very gentle with Gabriel and organised a christening at the church where Georgia had been christened. We had a party at home afterwards with family and godparents and friends. Then Mick took Gabriel and me off on a holiday to Turkey to stay with old friends. We were very happy together on that trip; we sang songs to baby Gabriel and laughed together. After our holiday Mick went back to the *Bridges to Babylon* tour, which travelled to 153 venues over a period of 20 months.

When Mick came back to London he looked very shaken. There was a newspaper report saying that Brazilian model Luciana Morad was pregnant with his baby. It was all too much for me to bear. I told him that I wanted a divorce.

At Anjelica Huston's wedding.

Becoming a Mum

Top left & Top right: My baby shower. The men, including Andy Warhol and Michael Chow, came along towards the end to pick everyone up and it turned into a bit of a cocktail party. Middle left: Just after the birth and Elizabeth Jagger poses for the camera for the first time. Middle right: Mick's mum and dad, Eva and Joe, and my Mama at Lizzie's christening. Bottom left: The proud mother. Bottom right: A delighted looking Mick with daughters Jade, Karis and little baby Elizabeth.

I always wanted children, and after Mick and I had been together for a few years, he agreed that we should try for a baby. I eventually conceived Elizabeth one rainy weekend while staying at a friend's cottage in Connecticut. I loved being pregnant, and my girlfriends gave me a fabulous baby shower. My sister Rosy arranged for a male stripper dressed as a policeman. Annie Leibovitz took the photos and at the end the guys arrived – including Andy Warhol and Fred, and it turned into a party. Elizabeth Scarlett Jagger was born on March 2, 1984. She weighed eight pounds and Mick was with me throughout. I took one look at her and was filled with overwhelming love. We christened her in England, with Mick's parents and my mother there.

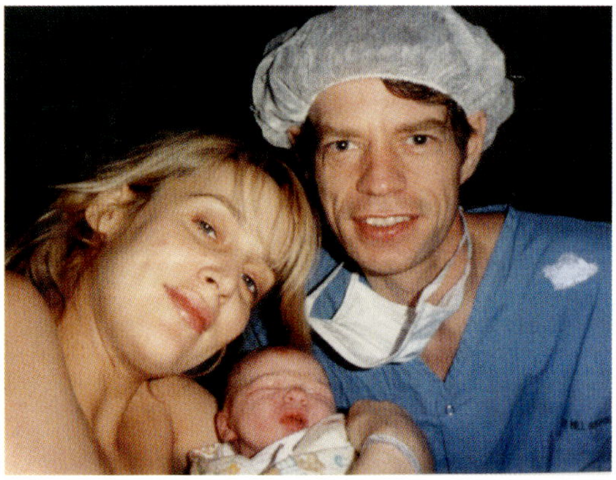

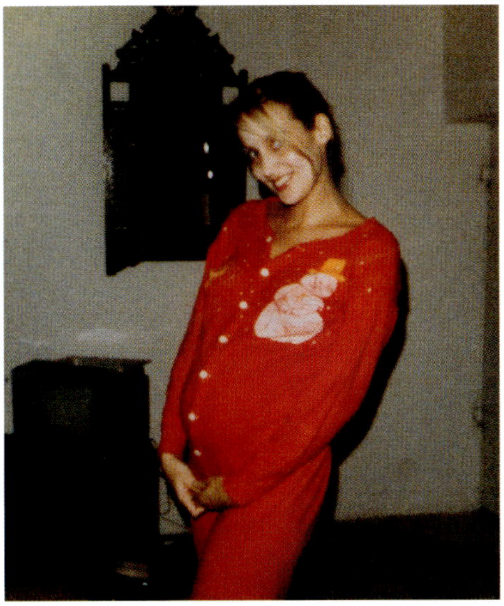

A year and a half later our next baby came along – James was born August 28th, 1985, healthy and gorgeous. His birth was all the more wonderful because during my pregnancy I had lost his twin. Once again I fell in love and Mick adored his son too. Mick was always sorry to be away from the children, and would send them little notes and drawings, to show he missed them. He adored our children and he was a wonderful father.

Top left: When I was pregnant I used to cover myself with olive oil so that I didn't get stretch marks. As a result all my clothes from that period had to be thrown out. **Top right:** Mick with James. **Bottom right:** Even though Mick was often away on tour, he would always send the children little drawings from wherever he was. **Following pages:** In Mustique we could be a normal family far away from the prying lenses of the paparazzi.

Mustique: Our Island Hideaway

Top right: In Mustique we could both be off duty, relax. We built a Japanese house as we wanted something that looked natural and didn't stand out.
Top left, Bottom left & Bottom right: Lazy afternoons spent out on the sea with the family were some of my favourite Mustique moments.

Mick and I loved Mustique, the tiny Caribbean Island where we could truly feel away from it all. We bought a stretch of beach there, and built a little Japanese-style house, with sliding doors and sleeping mats on the floor. Once we had the children, we went to our house in Mustique for Christmas and Easter. The island reminded me of my childhood in Texas. I loved the lush vegetation, the clear skies and the birds singing. It was still unspoilt and I felt so close to nature. I loved being barefoot on the dirt trails, and the way the air smelt after it rained. But best of all were the stars at night – they looked the way they had outside Gonzales at my grandmother's house. Being on the beach, we could hear the waves lapping at night, so soothing and beautiful.

Left: On the beach with Lizzie and Jimi. Below left: You can take a man away from his work... Below right: Catching the afternoon sun.

Left: Mick, Lizzie and Jimi up in the trees. **Below:** Me and Georgia May. **Opposite:** Piling in for a group hug.

The island was so small that everyone knew everyone and I felt it was safe for the children to roam about playing all day with the other children on the island, collecting seashells and catching crabs. It was one of the few places left in the world where the children could play outside with the freedom that my sisters and I had when we were growing up.

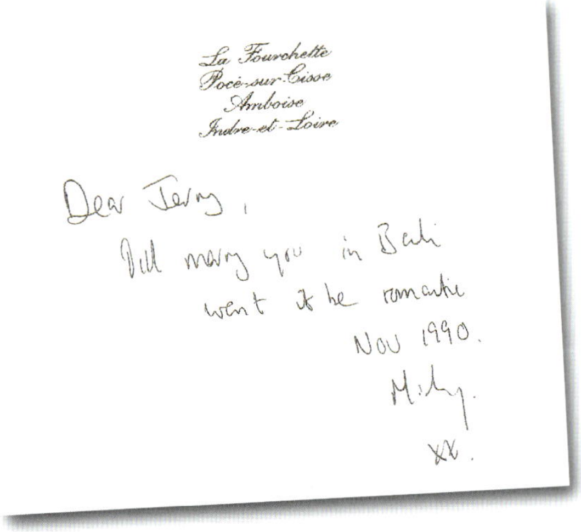
La Fourchette
Pocé-sur-Cisse
Amboise
Indre-et-Loire

Dear Jerry,
I'll marry you in Bali
won't it be romantic
Nov 1990.
Micky.
xx.

Our Exotic Wedding in Bali

In 1990, after years of waiting, Mick finally asked me to marry him!

I said yes, and we set off on a magical trip via Nepal, the tiny kingdom of Bhutan and Thailand. We took Elizabeth and James, then aged six and five, with us.

We both loved Bali and found it bewitching. We had been there on holiday and fallen in love with the beautiful Indonesian island, where the lush scenery and enchanting people made it feel like paradise. The people leave offerings of flowers and fruit not only at the temples, but everywhere, even by the road or next to a water pipe; anywhere that they think a spirit needs appeasing. The Balinese pursuit of wisdom is a national pastime and they have many festival days celebrating life with flowers and offerings and dances. The spices and the food are delicious and the people are always smiling and happy. The Balinese love children, we took Lizzie and Jimi to puppet shows and dances and everywhere we went the locals were so kind to them.

The wedding itself consisted of several ceremonies which went on throughout the day. It was in the village of Ubud, where the villagers had been decorating for days with an abundance of fresh flowers. It was a magical time; my only sadness was not having my family and friends with us. There were some bizarre moments – in one ceremony they killed chickens and poured blood on our feet – Lizzie and Jimi were horrified by that. The whole village was invited to the main ceremony, which went on for hours. At one point we acted out a scene where I was with the women and Mick came with the men and kidnapped me. Then we had a bath together in rose petals and then were dressed up in the most fantastic clothes. We drank champagne and had to do all sorts of rituals such as trading coconuts and Mick had to cut with a knife some fabric that I was holding to symbolise breaking the hymen. The high priest performed rituals with incense and put marks on our foreheads and blessed us. We signed a book and then sat on thrones on a stage and watched dancers perform. By the end of the day we were so tired!

The next morning Mick said he had to fly to Japan to collect an award. He took off, and I was left to bring the children, the nanny and the tutor and 20 or so suitcases back home to London. It wasn't quite the honeymoon I had hoped for!

Top: Everything about the wedding was a surprise, arranged by Mick. **Middle left, Middle centre & Middle right:** Getting into traditional Balinese dress for the ceremony. **Bottom left:** The final adjustments being made to my headdress. **Bottom right:** The ceremony in full swing.

90 11 13

The wedding was such a private affair that we didn't have a photographer. These snaps, taken by a friend, are not great quality, but they certainly bring back memories...

Happy Memories

When the tours and recording sessions ended, Mick and I would meet up and spend the holidays together with our children. Sometimes we went on exotic trips, elephant trekking in Nepal or game spotting in Kenya, but at other times we would just go to Mustique or Texas or France. I loved it when we were away – just our family, with no groupies chasing Mick and no phones ringing. We had such a lovely time together. In the heat of the day we would play gin rummy or backgammon or read books together, listening to all the birds singing their strange and different songs. Everywhere we went we bought things to take home: sarongs, beaded jewellery, beautiful cushions or ornaments. The children loved having time with us without other distractions – we went for walks, sang and played together, collected feathers and stones and made scrapbooks. Mick and I both loved the natural world and really were at our happiest in these remote places, with our children. At night we would sit outside and watch the stars and Mick would point out the constellations to the children, and I would see a shooting star and make a wish – that our life could continue like this.

We often took Jade and Karis with us when we went on holiday, so once Georgia and Gabriel had arrived we had six children in tow. Of course it could be a handful, but the older girls helped with the little ones and they all had each other as playmates. When we went to Texas, we met up with my mother, so that she could spend time with her grandchildren. She loved to see them and made the girls cute dresses. Sometimes we'd get together with Karis's mother Marsha, or with Jade's mother Bianca. I get on well with both of them; they're intelligent, interesting women and we have a lot in common.

Opposite left: One of many big family get togethers with Karis, Jade and Mick's parents. **Opposite right:** On holiday in Nepal. **Top right:** Georgia in her Easter bonnet. We always wore them in Texas and I kept this tradition going for my children. **Top left:** Movie club for the young ones (and a rather excited looking Jo Wood) backstage on a Stones tour. **Middle left:** Jimi, Georgia and a very fluffy bunny. **Middle right:** The family enjoying a picnic. **Bottom left:** Mick and Georgia May.

La Vie en Chateau

When we were working in Paris, we would escape to the Loire Valley at weekends, fantasizing about the lovely chateaux that were for sale, and eventually buying one of our own in 1984, close to the town of Amboise. It was called La Fourchette, which meant 'fork in the road'. It had been built in the sixteenth century for Louis XVI's finance minister. The chateau had a lot of land and was protected by a large stone wall and the river Loire. Behind the house was a tall limestone cliff with caves cut into it. We built a lake and I bought Mick two handmade wooden canoes. We used to go there with the children in the summer holidays and we had great fun rowing about on the lake and river. We also built a swimming pool and an impressive rose garden. In the small forest which was part of the estate we had bike trails and on top of the cliff we had vineyards. We would invite our friends and families and their children and had many wonderful times together. We all looked forward to going there, because it felt so safe and peaceful.

We would spend the days drifting idyllically on a barge down the Loire, drinking wine and eating picnics. We would all go on kayaks down the river, or on long bike rides through the forests and vineyards. Our party would sometimes be as many as 30 strong, including children of all ages, so it would require a great deal of organisation. We rented a big old bus to take us all on our outings and I was like a girl scout leader with my list, checking that we had everyone. I wore my hair in braids and was accused of being a bossy fraulein!

Above: Headscarf on and walking stick in hand, happily playing lord and lady of the manor. **Opposite:** A fairytale location like La Fourchette sometimes deserves a special arrival.

G-BNHW

While we had some blissfully peaceful and quiet family times at La Fourchette, playing with the children, or wandering quietly in the rose gardens, we loved to invite our friends to stay, and we had some wonderful times. Among our most frequent visitors were Bob Geldof and his children. They came the first summer after his wife Paula had run off with Michael Hutchence, in 1995 and she sadly passed away a few years later. Their story was a Modern Greek tragedy and we all tried our best to help them forget their heartache for a moment and remember how to live and laugh again.

Bob would read poetry to us girls in the small sitting room, while we would mend his torn shirts. He loved Burns and Byron and with his long unkempt hair and air of tragic loss, was incredibly romantic - all the girls had a crush on him. And of course he was a national hero who had single-mindedly forced the entire rock and roll world to raise millions to feed a starving and dying Africa and we were all very proud of him.

Above & Opposite: As well as being a beautiful place to live, La Fourchette was a beautiful location for photographic shoots. These shots were taken by renowned fashion photographer Guy Bourdin. **Right:** Racing through the gardens, with me bringing up last place!

Left & Above left: At La Fourchette we used to have some amazing parties, like this Moroccan themed one, often making good use of Mick's stage costumes, which he stored in the caves behind the house. **Above:** Our cross-dressing party was a particular hit with the men, who loved going through Mick's costumes and my closet too. Irritatingly many of the men fitted into my shoes. Mick wore my Manolo Blahniks – they were never the same again!

Top: Silly hats and a lunch party with Prince Rupert Loewenstein.
Left: A 16th century party to celebrate La Fourchette's 16th century origins.
Bottom middle & Bottom right: Some more snaps of our cross-dressing party. The 'ladies' definitely had the best time, behaving outrageously and enjoying their outfits immensely, while we girls had to fill their glasses!

Using my Assets at the Oxford Union

I was delighted when I was invited to speak in a debate at the Oxford University Union. I was following in the footsteps of some very distinguished company. Presidents, politicians and celebrities have addressed the Union in the past, so I knew I had to come up with a strong speech. The subject was: 'Should you use your assets, be it beauty, brains or brawn?'. I had Miss Russia, who was also Miss World, on my team, and opposing us they had some journalists.

Mick came with me, looking dazzling in black tie, which was the required dress, and all the kids came to see him and hear the debate. I really enjoyed writing my speech. I did it myself, but then I showed it to a couple of friends – Eric Idle from Monty Python and Ian La Frenais who wrote *Auf Wiedersehen Pet* and *Porridge* – and asked them to help me with a few jokes, because they always go down well. I used a quote from Benjamin Franklin; 'Hide not your talents, they for use were made. What's the use of a sundial in the shade?' My jokes went down extremely well – which wasn't surprising given the contributors. The best one was 'Time is only relative, it lasts a lot longer when your mother-in-law is there!' Then there was, 'To get on you must do the best you can with what fate has given you, or be really English and sit around moaning a lot about everyone else.' My conclusion was that, 'Our duty lies in the abundant use of our assets, provided that we take the care to use them wisely and considerately'. I had a very good time and we won the vote, which made us very happy and just a little bit smug!

Beauty uses her brains to win over Oxford Union

Marianne Macdonald listens as Jerry Hall quotes Socrates, Milton and her mother on exploiting your assets

JERRY HALL last night electrified Oxford Union by taking on feminists and former editors to argue it was everyone's duty to exploit their assets.

In the packed chamber she sat with Miss World (Julia Kurochkina), Melissa Bell (Lucy from *Neighbours*) and Mick Jagger. She wore a skin-tight, low-cut metallic dress, and the undergraduates' reaction suggested she had won the debate before it had even started.

Opposing the motion "This House believes it is the duty of everyone to exploit their assets, be they brains, beauty or brawn" were Louise Bagshawe, feminist and author; Mike Maloney, photographer of the year; and David Thomas, former editor of *Punch*.

Proposing the motion was Pete Gowers, secretary of the Union, who commended Melissa Bell as "the only character in *Neighbours* to have a surfboard named after her – because she's good for a ride, but not much else."

His opponents rolled out arguments including the examples of Asil Nadir, George Walker and Robert Maxwell as proof that exploitation of brains could lead, in the words of the Bible, to wailing and gnashing of teeth.

But the proposers had looks on their side. Julia Kurochkina, to huge applause, argued that beauty could get women jobs as air hostesses and secretaries, or into interviews "when they could then show their skills".

Melissa Bell said: "Journalists want to exploit me, so why shouldn't I exploit my assets?"

But the star of the evening was always going to be Jerry Hall. The supermodel had clearly done her research, citing in her 'if you've got it, flaunt it' argument sources as diverse as Milton, Socrates, Michelangelo, Helen of Troy and even Pasteur.

"My mother said to me when young you can catch more flies with honey than vinegar," she drawled. "I learned early on quite how far looks can get you. Why shouldn't we use our beauty?"

Causing ecstasy in the chamber, the supermodel then applauded the fact that her audience all had "good brains – some great bodies too", leaving only Mr Thomas to give her a run for her money.

"Jerry Hall once said a woman should be a great cook in the kitchen, a whore in bed and something else I've forgotten in the living room," he said. "Aside from the fact you might get confused and start quoting recipes in bed I can't agree. On this basis we could hardly be surprised if you were dropped for a better cook."

Jerry Hall looked unruffled. After all, Mick Jagger was beside her, proving that even fading supermodels can have the last laugh: as she certainly did when her side won the debate by 394 votes to 283.

Above: Cutting a dash on the way into the hall. **Left:** The Independent newspaper reporting on our victorious performance.

Sitting for Lucian Freud

When I was eight months pregnant with Gabriel, I sat next to Lucian Freud at dinner. He asked if he could paint me and wanted me to start the next day. I was flattered to be asked in my condition to model for such a great artist. I accepted and posed three times a week until I went into labour. I adored Lucian and felt cheered up to be involved in something creative. Although I was pregnant and posing nude, I felt so comfortable. Lucian adored my various lumps and bumps and, through his admiring eyes, I became very accepting of my growing body. It was so exhilarating to be appreciated for being natural and hugely pregnant. That was a great gift Lucian gave me. He was so interested in how I felt and would put his hand on my stomach and feel the baby kick and get excited. He seemed to be doing all the things that my husband should have been doing. When I complained about Mick, Lucian said to me, 'Never leave your husband, he works hard, pays the bills and leaves you alone. He's the perfect husband!' Maybe he would have been if I hadn't minded so much.

Lucian loved poetry and, like me, knew a lot of it by heart. We passed the time taking turns reciting poems to each other. I still remembered a lot of the Edgar Allan Poe I had read as a child and Lucian loved it. He admired the poetry of Rochester, which I found very provocative. We talked a lot about art, and he was very impressed that I had been so close to Andy Warhol. He loved Warhol's work and rated him as a truly innovative artist. He also loved David Hockney, who we met for lunch, but his favourite artist and best friend was Frank Auerbach.

Lucian was pleased with the way that I could get back into exactly the same position with the same angles. He told me that very few people could do that, and that I made a very good artist's model. I was used to holding the same position for long periods of time and loved the peace and tranquillity of Lucian's studio: no phones rang and no one ever rang the doorbell.

Lucian told such good stories. He told me that when he was quite young, he had shared a flat, a bed and a redhead with the poet Dylan Thomas. We both adored Johnny Cash and would talk about his songs. Sometimes Lucian would drive us in his gold Rolls Royce to have lunch at the River Café. We stayed friends and after Gabriel's birth I took him along in his carry-cot and we met for delicious lunches.

Above: 'Eight Months Gone' by Lucian Freud, 1997.

Left: One of the last times that Mick and I were photographed in public together before the divorce. Right: Mick and me, Cap D'Antibes, 1991 by Helmut Newton (reproduced from an original tearsheet).

End of the Affair

Breaking up with Mick was painful, in so many ways. We had been together for 23 years when, shortly after Gabriel's birth, I discovered that Mick was having a child with someone else. Of course he hadn't planned it – he was shocked when he heard. But it was the final straw for me. I had put up with his infidelities, but having a child with another woman was simply too much. I had been tempted to leave Mick many times and had never done it, but this time I asked him for a divorce.

The most difficult part was telling the children. But I spoke to them and told them we loved them and that we were still their parents. It wasn't easy at first, but now I am able to look back and think that I was with Mick for all those years and we had four children and the fact that we stayed together so long and made such a wonderful family was an amazing success. We still loved each other and were determined that, even though our marriage had ended, we would continue to be parents together – and we have. We were always great friends and we still are. We speak often and Mick comes to visit and spends as much time as he can with the children.

Summer Holiday

It's August
The time passes bearable enough
Now that my sister comes

I swim and read, eat and drink
Paint and play cards and write and
Dead head the roses

Far away
Another woman holidays
With my children

Opposite: Me in my favourite role as Mrs. Robinson in the Graduate, London, 2001.

10

SINGLE GIRL

Enjoying my freedom

When Mick and I settled in London we moved into a beautiful house on the edge of Richmond Park, on a hill overlooking the winding Thames River. Our house was built in 1750 and has large rooms with tall ceilings. Lizzie and Jimi went to a local school, a five-minute drive through Richmond Park. I loved the house and had fun decorating it with the brilliant designer David Mlinaric and laying out the garden with Alvida Lees-Milne.

Today I still live in the same house, and although my life is very different now, I am happier than I have ever been. The wonderful thing about getting older is that you become grateful for the simple blessings in life. Maybe it is because of the harder times that have passed. Now I wake up happy, I go downstairs and let the dogs out and make a cup of coffee. I collect my lovely warm brown eggs that the chickens have laid and I get my children up for school.

I love being a stay at home Mom and picking and choosing the work I do. My two youngest children are still at home, Lizzie spends a lot of time in New York, but when she's in England she stays in the small cottage we have at the bottom of the garden. And Jimi is across London in Camden, but he comes home a lot, and we all try to have Sunday lunch together every week.

I feel blessed to have had such an interesting and varied career. Over the past few years I have been able to develop my acting career and I've loved taking some really challenging theatre roles. Fame isn't always easy – if I'm in the West End then every few minutes someone comes up and wants an autograph or wants to say something to me, so it can be a little frustrating, but I know the people who come to talk are the theatre-going public and are genuinely interested. It's just tough on anyone I'm with, as we can never finish a conversation. But I know I've been enormously lucky and I'm grateful people are so kind, supportive and interested.

The Hall girls outside the Louvre in Paris.

I've also taken an Open University degree and been studying poetry through The Arvon Foundation. I did a poetry reading at the Ledbury Poetry Festival and the audience was lovely; mostly older people and a few hippies. I took my twin sister Terry with me and we all had tea afterwards and discussed poetry.

Terry has spent the last few years with me in the south of France, where I bought a house. We swim and play cards and write poetry together. I feel it's such a luxury to have the time to daydream and write poetry.

Mick and I get on well and are able to talk on very friendly terms about our four children's welfare. Of course, I still love him, how can you un-love? But, thankfully we have both moved on. After the divorce the children and I spent the first summer in the south of France. Our great friends, Dave Stewart of the Eurythmics and photographer Anoushka Fisz were getting married on the beach near my new house. Mick came, and spent the night of the party in my guest room. The next day he went off with his camera crew in tow – he was making a documentary of his life. I waved goodbye and thought how lucky I was that I didn't care what he got up to anymore. It was no longer my problem.

With Prince Charles at the Glass Slipper Ball in aid of Lodon's Hackney Empire theatre.

I am also good friends with his other exes; Marsha and Bianca. I'm friends with Mick's current partner too, L'Wren. To be honest, I think she's better at dealing with him than I am. He needs a lot of adoration, which I wasn't really willing to give him.

Marsha is amazing, she's very clever, very funny and she's written lots of books. She came with me to plant my son James' garden recently; we spent all day planting flowers. We are like a big extended family.

I don't do a lot of modelling these days, but I loved working with Karl Lagerfeld in 2009 on his Chanel accessories range. I am also involved in a lot of charities to do with children. It's nice to be able to give something back. And I've become an agony aunt for *The Times* newspaper, and have made several radio programmes for the BBC and Radio 4.

Rock stars are like sailors in that they spend large amounts of time away, leaving their womenfolk at home. We girls tended to keep each other company and we've stayed close. My great rock chick girlfriends include Jo Wood, Jeanne Marine (Bob Geldof's partner), Rachel Fuller (Pete Townsend's partner), and Suzanne Wyman, who is my best friend. We sometimes get together with our creative writing group called The Butterfly Club, named after little butterfly rings that I gave the girls. We take turns reading bits from our books, plays and poetry.

I've been an ambassador for the Prince's Trust for over twenty years. I'm a big fan of Prince Charles. The charity helps disadvantaged young people to find direction and I turn up at events and host fundraising shows. My children have worked for the Trust too; Jimi helped them with scouting locations for a film.

I can't imagine not being based in England now. I still love to visit France in the holidays though, and of course I go back to the States to see my friends and family.

Mick and I talk often and we meet up at parties now and then. He comes over to see the children and he has them for the summer holidays. It's good not to mind, to have moved on.

Top left: In rehearsal with director Terry Johnson and Josh Cohen.
Opposite: On-stage as Mrs. Robinson.
Following pages: At a press launch for The Graduate – the play received a lot of media attention and Mick came to support me at the premiere.

Here's to you Mrs. Robinson

It was not until Gabriel was a year old and I found myself newly divorced that I returned to the theatre. The producers Sacha Brooks and John Reid asked me to audition for the part of Mrs. Robinson in *The Graduate*. I had seen Kathleen Turner in the play and had loved it; it was so powerful and funny. Terry Johnson had written the adaptation and was directing it. I read for the part and was hired. I was so nervous, I hadn't been in a play for quite a while, and this one involved being nude onstage. But I ended up loving the experience. I adored Terry and we played to packed houses who roared with laughter.

In order to play a character you need to have empathy for them; to understand why they say what they do and what motivates them. Mrs. Robinson is a frustrated alcoholic who seduces her friend's son, Benjamin. Her husband is away working a lot so she's lonely. But she's frustrated too. She had studied art in school but had never been creative. She says awful things to her daughter, but I think she is afraid that her daughter will give up on her dreams too. She doesn't want to talk to Benjamin or have any sort of emotional connection; she just wants blind sex. I think she is ashamed of her behaviour. There is also something deeper and darker to it – maybe some infringement of boundaries from her past. These kinds of musings give a character an inner life and keep an actor interested throughout a long run. And the thing I find most fascinating is that when relating to the character you stumble on issues within your own past that can be worked through also.

I played Mrs. Robinson for six months in the West End and then toured North America with the play for another five months. We played in my hometown Austin, Texas, and my mother, sisters and relatives all came to see it. In 2010 I took it to Australia for six weeks.

The Graduate
'THE GRADUATE IS SUPERB!
KATHLEEN TURNER
is every bit a star
and delivers
TELEPHONE

EVENING OF IMPURE
EATRICAL DELIGHT'
Evening Standard
'THE GRADUATE SENSATION!
KATHLEEN TURNER,
the Hollywood film
star who started
never lost
of sexual
Evening Standard

Theatre

In the last few years I've done quite a bit of theatre. After *The Graduate* I was in *The Vagina Monologues* in the West End and on a North American tour. Again we went to Texas and my mother said, 'First you show it and now you talk about it!'

My next play was another comedy, *The Play What I Wrote*, directed by Kenneth Branagh. It was so much fun to do. Over-the-top Morecambe and Wise humour, and Kenneth is so handsome and a wonderfully relaxed director. The stars of the play were Toby Jones and Hamish McColl, and they were brilliant. We toured England and went to Belfast, too.

After that I did a tour of England playing in *Picasso's Women*, a 52-minute monologue directed by Andy Jordan. It was a wonderfully moving play, all about the naughty, dark side of Pablo Picasso, but it was stressful having so many lines to remember. My next play, at the New End Theatre in Hampstead, was *Benchmark*, directed by Michael Rudman. Michael had written it with Bud Shrake, who is also from Texas.

Left: Jumping around on-stage in one of my least-flattering costumes in The Play What I Wrote, 2002. **Opposite top right:** With my fellow castmates Ruth Madoc and Nikki Sanderson for The Vagina Monologues, 2006. **Opposite bottom right:** On-stage in Benchmark, 2002.

Candida
Benson
Jerry
Hall
Picasso's
Women
By Brian McAvera
Cherie
Lunghi
Gwen
Taylor
Frances
Tomelty

Ismail Merchant came to see me in *The Graduate* and he gave me a part in his 2002 film *Merci Docteur Rey*, directed by Andrew Litvack and starring Jane Birkin. I had a drunk scene in *The Graduate* and everyone said I did a drunk really well; it's quite hard to do, so Ismail asked me to play an alcoholic in this film. We filmed in Paris and Ismail was so sweet and cooked a delicious dinner for us. After that I had great fun filming a children's movie called *Tooth* – about the tooth fairy. I played the wife of Richard E. Grant who is a neighbour and friend. My children loved it and were very proud of me.

I also entered the *Guinness Book of World Records* in 2004 for performing in six West End plays in one night; *Les Miserables*, *The Phantom of the Opera*, *Fame*, *Blood Brothers*, *Chitty Chitty Bang Bang* and *Anything Goes*. Theatre in London really suffered after 9/11, so this was a publicity stunt designed to encourage tourists back into the West End. I was thrilled to do it but it took a huge amount of planning and preparing. I had to travel from theatre to theatre on the back of a motorcycle, wear clothes under clothes and rush onto stage on cue each time. My children were really proud of that, and my record still hasn't been broken.

Above: One of many promotional shots for Calendar Girls, sunflowers strategically placed. **Opposite top:** Reclining on a chaise longue and playing a very convining drunk in Ismail Merchant's Merci Docteur Rey. **Opposite bottom:** Ready to spend a night whizzing across London's West End in my bid to enter the Guinness Book of World Records.

My most recent play was *Calendar Girls*, which was a huge success. I played Celia and really enjoyed working with the rest of the feisty cast.

TOTALLY
LONDON
TOTALLY
LONDON
TOTALLY
LONDON

Vivienne Westwood

Vivienne has always been one of my favourite designers. I first got to know her in the seventies when Punk was at its height: she and her then partner Malcolm McLaren ran Sex, a cult clothes shop on the King's Road. Vivienne, through her great knowledge of history and incredible talent as a craftswoman, had forged her own new and exciting vision of how women should dress. What I love most about Vivienne's clothes is her humour – from her sex shop to her fig leaves and her crazy tartan suits, she is always entertaining. Her husband, Andreas, a former fashion student of hers, is also very talented. They've been good friends to me and the girls, giving Lizzie modelling opportunities at an early age.

Vivenne's clothes are sexy, flattering and well-cut. For an older woman, I think she's virtually the only designer you can wear. You still look sexy but you don't look as if you're trying to look too young. She's one of the only designers I want to wear now; I know I'm safe in Vivienne Westwood. I do like some of the Chanel stuff, but all the other clothes I think 'no, not good'.

When I modelled for Vivienne she always had a story to go with the clothes. With this beautiful black gown she said, 'Right, you're an aristocratic Englishwoman, you live in a big run-down house, you've got no money; you're eccentric and you're wearing your ballgown to tea'. And I knew exactly what she wanted!

Above middle: On the runway for Vivienne Westwood at Paris Fashion Week, 2001. **Above right:** Modelling Vivienne's pret-a-porter collection, 1997. **Opposite:** Chanelling my inner mad English aristocrat in one of Vivienne's sumptuous ball gowns.

Karl Lagerfeld

In 2009 Karl asked me to appear in his Chanel accessory campaign, which was very flattering. The campaign was based on the story of Cheri from the novel by Collette about an older courtesan who has a much younger lover. I think perhaps Karl got the idea of asking me after seeing *The Graduate*. It was certainly very flattering at my age to be asked to do a modelling campaign with Karl Lagerfeld. I've known him since I was 16; we've had a long relationship. He's a great photographer, too. In the advertisements I'm in my lingerie, but it's such beautiful, sensual lingerie, not too revealing and very flattering, too. I do think Karl makes exquisite clothes for older women; you always look good in Chanel classics, although they're expensive.

I first met Karl through Antonio, who used to be his boyfriend; they hung out before Karl was famous, and then he went on to be the biggest designer. Like Thierry Mugler, a lot of his references are from old Hollywood movies. I know them and so do my children because I always made them watch all these old movies with Bette Davis and Mae West, Marlene Dietrich and Veronica Lake. Karl will say, 'O.K., you're Bette Davis in *The Letter*', and if you've seen it you know exactly what he wants. That's the one thing I said to my daughters; you've got to watch all the old Hollywood movies because they really did glamour and everything you need to know about modelling is in there. Lizzie worked for Karl at one point and she sai,d 'Mum it was so great, because he talked about the old movies and I knew what pose to do and he said "Oh my God, you're the only young model I've worked with who knows what I'm talking about"'. Movie stars are no longer iconic and glamorous, which is such a shame; there's no equivalent now.

Left: With Karl Lagerfeld at a Chanel Spring/Summer haute couture fashion show. **Opposite:** I adore this shot that Karl took of me for his 2009 Chanel campaign. I don't do much modelling these days, but when someone like Karl asks you to front a campaign for him it's an honour.

CHANEL
31, RUE CAMBON

The Proud Mother

I think my greatest achievement is being a good mother and raising my four wonderful, caring, creative and thoughtful children. I'm hugely proud of all of them. My three oldest are grown up now – Lizzie and Georgia are modelling and Jimi is an actor and musician. Gabriel is at school and isn't interested in fame, he wants to be a history teacher, like Mick's father.

My stepdaughters are wonderful women too. Karis and Jade each have two children, so I'm a step-grandmother and I love it. Family has always been so important to me, and I still get together with my mother and sisters whenever I can and whenever we do, it's a hoot. Terry and I still talk a couple of times a week. Her kids are the same age as Lizzie and Jimi and they're all very close.

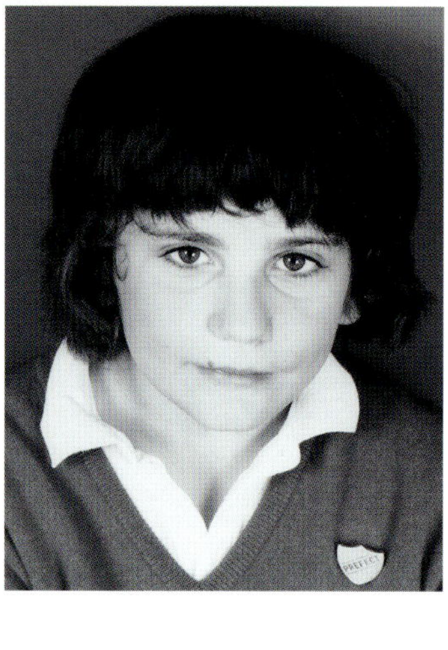

Far left: Lizzie modelling for Lancôme. **Top left:** Jimi's acting mugshot. **Bottom left:** A school portrait of Gabriel. **Opposite:** Georgia May and me in a shoot that we did for Invisible Zinc suncream, 2010.

PICTURE CREDITS

The images used within this book are the private property and copyright of the author, unless stated otherwise. The publisher would like to thank the following photographers, agencies and companies for their kind permission to reproduce the photographs in this book:

2 Photograph by Lichfield/Commissioned by The Mandarin Oriental Hotel Group for their global Fan advertising campaign; 4 above right Media Press/Rex Features, centre above left: Graham Hughes, centre above right Richard Young/Rex Features, centre below left © Annie Leibovitz, 2010 (image reproduced from Polaroid), centre below right The Kobal Collection/Warner Bros/DC Comics, below right © Pierre Vauthey/Corbis Sygma; 6 Timothy Greenfield-Sanders; 8-9 Barry Lategan/The Condé Nast Publications Ltd., Trunkarchive.com; 24 photograph by Suze, Camera Press London; 29 photograph by Suze, Camera Press London; 30 Photographs by Hans Fuerer; 32-34 Antonio Lopez; 35 Norman Parkinson Archive; 36-37 Antonio Lopez; 39 French Vogue, Paris, Autumn/Winter 1974 © The Helmut Newton Estate; 40 © The Helmut Newton Estate; 41 French Vogue, Paris, Autumn/Winter 1974 © The Helmut Newton Estate; 42 © The Helmut Newton Estate/Maconochie Photography; 44-45 © The Helmut Newton Estate/Maconochie Photography; 47 © The Helmut Newton Estate/Maconochie Photography; 48 Opium Perfume Campaign, Yves Saint Laurent © the Helmut Newton Estate; 49 Yves Saint Laurent Rive Gauche Campaign © the Helmut Newton Estate; 50 above SIPA Press/Rex Features; 50 below SIPA Press/Rex Features; 51 left AFP/Getty Images; 51 right © Reuters/Philippe Wojazer; 52 Media Press/Rex Features; 56 Archive Photos/Getty Images; 57 Media Press/Rex Features; 58 Courtesy of Cosmopolitan/Hearst © Francesco Scavullo; 59 © Francesco Scavullo; 60 © The Richard Avedon Foundation; 63 Horst P. Horst/Art + Commerce; 64-65 Courtesy of Arthur Elgort; 66 Gunter Sachs; 69 Jerry Hall, Saint Martin 1975 © HIRO 1975, photo courtesy of HIRO; 70 right photograph Bill King; 71 February 1976/Harper's Bazaar, photograph Bill King; 72-73 May 1979/Harper's Bazaar, photograph Bill King; 74-75 courtesy of Neiman Marcus; 76-79 May/June 1975, Vogue Patterns photographs Steven Horn; 80-81 © Norman Parkinson/Sygma/Corbis; 82-85 Norman Parkinson Archive; 86 Photo David Bailey; 89 Graham Hughes; 92-94 Graham Hughes; 95 above and below Graham Hughes; 95 right Roxy Music 'Siren' 1975, Cover by Jerry Hall, Bryan Ferry, Graham Hughes, Anthony Price, Nicholas de Ville, Bob Bowkett, Celine, Adrianne Hunter. Produced by Chris Thomas for E. G. Records Ltd.; 98 www.brianaris.com; 99 Photo David Bailey/Vogue ©The Condé Nast Publications Ltd.; 101 HaneKroot/Redferns/Getty Images; 102 www.brianaris.com; 105 Mirrorpix; 106 Richard Young/Rex Features; 107 Photo David Bailey/Tatler ©The Condé Nast Publications Ltd.; 108-111 Photo David Bailey; 112-113 Sipa Press/Rex Features; 114 Mirrorpix; 115 © Bettmann/Corbis; 116 Willem Diepraam; 118 Norman Parkinson Archive; 119 Norman Parkinson/Vogue ©The Condé Nast Publications Ltd.; 120 - 127 Norman Parkinson Archive; 128 Richard Young/Rex Features; 134 courtesy of Arthur Elgort; 136 Ken Regan/Camera 5; 138-139 Linda Matlow/Rex Features; 141 above right, below left Ken Regan/Camera 5; 142 below right Ken Regan/Camera 5; 144 Alan Davidson; 145 above Alan Davidson; 145 below Galella/WireImage/Getty Images; 146 Norman Parkinson Archive; 157 © Wally McNamee/Corbis; 158-159 © George Hurrell Estate; 161 Mick Jagger/Vogue Paris ©The Condé Nast Publications Ltd.; 162 Sipa Press/Rex Features; 163 Interview cover: July 1978, photographed by Peter Strongwater. Designed and painted by Richard Bernstein.; 164-165 Platzer/Time & Life/Getty Images; 167 © The Andy Warhol Foundation for the Visual Arts/Corbis/Artists Rights Society (ARS), New York / DACS, London 2010; 168 HultonArchive/Getty Images; 170-171 Alan Davidson; 172 Courtesy of Patrick Demarchelier; 175 Alan Davidson; 176-177 Photo David Bailey; 178 Photo David Bailey; 181 & 182-183 © Terence Donovan Archive, Courtesy of Terence Donovan Archive; 184 photograph by Patrick Lichfield; 185 photograph by Patrick Lichfield; 186 Alan Davidson; 187 above left, below left and below right Alan Davidson; 187 above right and centre right Richard Young/Rex Features; 188-189 Alan Davidson; 190 Alan Davidson; 191 Richard Young/Rex Features; 193 left ITV/Rex Features; 193 right NBCUPHOTOBANK/Rex Features; 194 The Kobal Collection/Warner Bros/DC Comics; 195 The Official comic adaptation of the Warner Bros. motion picture BATMAN © 1989 DC Comics Inc. Writer: Dennis O'Neill, Artist: Jerry Ordway with colour artist Steve Oliff; 196 Lyric Theatre;197 above left and above right Mirrorpix; 197 centre left Platzer/Time & Life/Getty Images; 197 below left Richard Young/Rex Features; 197 below right Peter Brooker/Rex Features; 198 © Annie Leibovitz, 2010 (reproduced from Polaroid); 199 © Annie Leibovitz, 2010; 200 © Richard Melloul/Sygma/Corbis; 201 Catalogue: Theirry Mugler Collection A/W 1996/1997, Photographer: Thierry Mugler; Hair: Paolo Ferreira; Make Up: Carole Lasnier pour CLARINS; 202-203 'Angel' Campaign 1995 Thierry Mugler; 204 © Norman Parkinson/Sygma/Corbis; 209 © Philip Ramey/Sygma/Corbis; 214 above right Photograph by Isabel Snyder, Mustique, 1991; 216 Photograph by Isabel Snyder, Mustique, 1991; 219 below left Sipa Press/Rex Features; 226 & 227 above ©Estate of Guy Bourdin/Art + Commerce; 231 The Independent; 233 Courtesy: Lucian Freud Archive; © The Helmut Newton Estate/Maconochie Photography; 236 Alwyn R Coates/alwynphoto.com; 239 Sun/Rex Features; 240 Alastair Muir; 241 Nigel Norrington/ArenaPAL; 242-243 David Sandison/The Independent; 244 Richard Young/Rex Features; 245 left Churchill Theatre, Bromley; 245 above Huw John/Rex Features; 245 below Geraint Lewis/The Independent; 246 John Swannell/David Pugh Ltd.; 247 above The Kobal Collection/Merchant Ivory/Eat Your Soup; 247 below Getty Images Entertainment; 248 left © CARDINALE STEPHANE/Corbis Sygma; 248 centre Steve Wood/Rex Features; 248 right © Photo B.D.V./Corbis; 249 Mirrorpix; 250 © Pierre Vauthey/Corbis Sygma; 252 left Mert Alas & Marcus Piggot; 253 Jerry Hall for Invisible Zinc. Photo Jonas Bresnan.

The publisher has made every effort to trace the copyright holders. We apologise in advance for any unintentional omissions and would be pleased to insert the appropriate acknowledgment in any subsequent edition.

ACKNOWLEDGEMENTS

I would like to give special thanks to Simon Kelner, Rosemary Goad and my good friend Robert Lacey for their encouragement and support in writing this book; to Caro Handley who helped me edit and craft the text to the photographs; also to my assistant and typist Bernie Kilmartin.

A big thank you to my agent, Jonathan Phang, who persuaded me to do the book and helped with the huge task of selecting the photographs; to Fenton Bailey for scanning endless images onto discs; to Mike Trow and Brett Croft from British *Vogue* for their encyclopaedic knowledge and to David Bailey, June Newton (and Tiggy Maconochie) for so generously supplying their photographs as a personal favour.

From my publishers, Quadrille, I would like to thank Anne Furniss, who pushed me to make this book as good as I could, as well as to Simon Davis and David Rowley for their dedication and skill.

Above all, I give grateful and heartfelt thanks to all the great photographers whose beautiful work is reproduced in this book.

For my children – Elizabeth, James, Georgia and Gabriel

First published in 2010 by
Quadrille Publishing Limited,
Alhambra House,
27–31 Charing Cross Road,
London WC2H 0LS

Editorial Director: **Anne Furniss**
Creative Director: **Helen Lewis**
Project Editor: **Simon Davis**
Designer: **David Rowley**
Production Director: **Vincent Smith**
Production Controller: **Aysun Hughes**

Cataloguing in Publication data:
a catalogue reference for this book
is available from the British Library.

ISBN 978 184400 880 3

Printed in China